Metaphors & Analogies

Power Tools
for Teaching Any Subject

Rick Wormeli

Stenhouse Publishers
Portland, Maine

Stenhouse Publishers
www.stenhouse.com

Credits
page 59: Figure 5.2 adapted from "Emancipating the English Language Learner" by Rick Wormeli, in the April 2009 issue of *Middle Ground* (pp. 41–42). Adapted with permission from National Middle School Association.
page 70: Figure 6.1a and b appears courtesy of Charlene Lam (www.charlenelam .com). Reprinted with permission.
page 79: Figure 7.1 appears courtesy of Norm Blumenthal. Reprinted with permission.
page 91: Figure 7.3 from *A Visual Approach to Algebra* by Frances Van Dyke, © 1998 Pearson Education, Inc. or its affiliates. Used by permission.

Library of Congress Cataloging-in-Publication Data
Wormeli, Rick.
    Metaphors & analogies : power tools for teaching any subject / Rick Wormeli.
        p. cm.
        Includes bibliographical references and index.
        ISBN 978-1-57110-758-9 (alk. paper)
        1. Teaching. 2. Metaphor—Study and teaching. I. Title. II. Title: Metaphors and analogies.
        LB1025.3.W725 2009
        371.39—dc22
                                                            2009019943

Cover design, interior design, and typesetting by Martha Drury

Manufactured in the United States of America
PRINTED ON 30% PCW
RECYCLED PAPER

15 14 13 12 11 10 09   9 8 7 6 5 4 3 2

For educators who seek meaningful metaphors to improve instruction,
create new metaphors when the current ones don't serve,
and inspire others to do the same

Contents

v

Acknowledgments

'd like to replace the words *integrity* and *inspiration* with two people: Holly Holland and John Herzfeld. These two are the collective push and muse every writer needs. This book would not exist without their vision for what it could become. They've forgiven my immature first attempts, asked candid questions to confront shaky thinking, and provided direction when I was lost. On more than one occasion, I considered what they would expect from worthy writing on this topic and then unfolded the map this reflection provided and wrote like my mind was on fire. I am in their debt and still haven't cooled off.

Philippa Stratton, Dan Tobin, Chris Downey, Erin Trainer, Chandra Lowe, Nate Butler, Bill Varner, Jay Kilburn, Chuck Lerch, Zsofia McMullin, Rebecca Eaton, and everyone else at Stenhouse Publishers continue to elevate writing and education above the cynics' reach, turning out quality book after quality book. I am grateful for every thumbs-up I get from them, and I want to be worthy of their consideration in all efforts.

The MiddleTalk Listserv and Teacher Leaders Network (TLN) are the living metaphors for generosity and professionalism. The conversations in each Listserv inspire much of my direction as an educator. Many thanks to those of you who post on these sites. You lift all of us worldwide when you do. Speaking of those who lift others with their creativity and dedication, special thanks to Dr. Debbie Silver and Todd Williamson for their lengthy contributions of metaphorical thinking to this book.

Thank you, too, to the students who responded to their teachers' requests to provide samples for this new book on metaphors and analogies. You've made the book ten times better as a result.

Thinkers, athletes, and musicians Ryan and Lynn Wormeli are two of the coolest people you'll ever meet. They are clearly on their way to out-achieve their father in every respect, and I couldn't be more proud of them or grateful they let me come along for the ride.

Most of all, thanks go to my wife, Kelly, who provides the stability and logistics within our family so that I am able to come out and play in this sandbox. She's a remarkable woman in her own right, a phenomenon as a wife and mother.

*A picture is worth a thousand words, but the right metaphor is worth
a thousand pictures.*
—Daniel Pink, 2008

Every age has a keyhole to which its eye is pasted.
—Mary McCarthy, 1953

*An individual's creation of metaphor is part of a fundamental human
impulse to find meaning in life. . . . Through its capacity to clarify meaning
in complex settings, metaphor is able to go beyond the limitations of
scientific languages and description.*
—Eugene F. Provenzo Jr., 1989

Events Create Ripples and Equations Are Balances: Metaphors in Every Subject

From a high school teacher:

I asked my ninth-grade class to deconstruct a metaphor in their read-ing. They were stumped and silent. Thinking to myself, what's the dif-ference between a metaphor and a simile, I backtracked a bit. I asked the class if the United States were an animal, what animal would it be and why?

Total uncomfortable silence. We all squirmed while I looked at the board and thought: Okay, what animal am I going to pick? What com-parisons am I going to make?

As I turned back to the class, Pete, a special education student, had his hand waving in the air.

"If the U.S.A. were an animal," he said, "it would be a big dog that likes to be on the porch. But once that dog gets riled, look out—it will come off that porch looking for a fight. But most of the time it likes to take it easy, it likes being on that porch with all the other dogs looking at it."

Pete was known for being a goof in class, so several kids started to laugh. But he continued quickly and confidently: "No, no, really you guys; look at us. Look at what we've been studying this year. The U.S.

didn't want to get involved in World War I or World War II. We wanted to stay home. We're the richest country; we get to stay on the porch, no rain on us, no snow."

I looked at the class. Students were nodding their heads. Everybody was looking at Pete.

"Look at what we're doing in Kosovo," he continued. "We like being the boss, but we don't want to get off the porch to do it."

After class, I told Pete what a nice job he had done explaining his metaphor. I said I thought most students got the comparisons he made, but most of them found it really hard to construct metaphors on their own.

"Hard?" he said. "Hell! That was about the easiest thing you've had me do all year. Any time you want me to compare stuff like that, I'm your guy."

So there I was with this totally new insight into Pete, a boy who struggled to read and write but made comparisons far more sophisticated and concise than students who read and wrote with far more facility than he ever would.

As teachers, we live for such aha! moments: those times when our lessons evoke an "Oh, I get it now!" euphoria in students. It might be a lab demonstration, a successfully completed math problem, or a series of guiding questions that eventually lead to understanding and make a lasting connection.

What was the difference? How did we get their mental gears in sync? When we look back over our most successful lessons, we realize that these mini-epiphanies often occur in the presence of metaphors and analogies:

- ⚡ "In this situation, Prussia was a cornered mountain lion."
- ⚡ "This molecule is trying to flirt with that other molecule."
- ⚡ "What does *irrational* mean when it is used to describe human behavior? Let's see if that description applies to irrational numbers in math."

On other occasions, students fail to thrive because they cannot grasp the metaphor we have chosen, or because we let an opportunity to build a bridge to understanding slip away. "If only I had a good analogy that would have cleared this up for these students," we lament as we grade their less-than-successful papers. "What do you mean that you don't see how a Mercator projection is like a peeled orange—Didn't I explain it well enough?"

Little in education has as much influence on students' academic and personal success as the metaphors and analogies teachers use to make unfamiliar concepts clear. Given their significance, metaphors and analogies should be one of the primary considerations in lesson design.

Today's classrooms are fertile ground for constructive use of comparisons. Metaphors and analogies can be used to shape our thinking, and thereby our actions, but they can also open our minds to new ideas unattainable through other means:

- ⚡ In music class, students perceive the intricate melody of a new piece of music as someone running up stairs, stumbling down a few steps then leaping forward to an airy emancipation from gravity.
- ⚡ In algebra class, students finally understand equations because they see either side of the equal sign as extended bars on balance.
- ⚡ In biology class, the complexity of the Krebs cycle gets simplified when someone explains it as an energy processing factory for Citric Acid, made of six smaller interactions working together that create ATP (adenosine triphosphate).

For more examples of metaphors from successful classroom teachers, see Appendix B in the back of this book.

Purposefully Teaching with Metaphors

Mathematics is not a way of hanging numbers on things so that quantitative answers to ordinary questions can be obtained. It is a language that allows one to think about extraordinary questions . . . getting the picture does not mean writing out the formula or crunching the numbers, it means grasping the mathematical metaphor.
—James Bullock, 1994

Formally teaching through metaphors and their main subset, analogies, represents a different way of teaching for many. Some of us make good comparisons routinely and naturally: When a student seems confused, we think of something related to their personal lives. "T.J., you like working on cars, so let's compare how a car's engine regulates internal temperature with the way mammals regulate internal temperature. Then we'll compare it with how reptiles do it, which is very different." The student says, or at least thinks, "Now, I get it," and we move on—though we stop periodically and make sure that he really does.

For others, learning how to use appropriate metaphors or how to guide students to create their own unique metaphors will require adjustments in thinking and curricular planning. How do we frame meaning? That's a much different question than, Will we get through Chapter 10 by the midterm exam?

What may need to change in many of our classrooms is the purposeful pursuit of metaphors and analogies in our teaching instead of the momentary inspirations that may or may not be helpful to students' learning. We don't want to leave such effective strategies to chance.

Teaching through metaphors and analogies isn't just about building personal background knowledge so students have a context for understanding new concepts. Nor is it just about giving students templates to complete (_____ is to _____ as _____ is to _____) or assigning students to compare and contrast two periods of history or pieces of literature. It's also a conscious choice to scaffold learning by making meaningful connections among topics. By giving students specific tools to think critically, such as making the invisible visible through explicit comparisons or applying knowledge from one discipline to another, we help students move beyond memorization to deeper learning that lasts.

Not Just in English Class

It's time to bust metaphors out of solitary confinement in English classes. Many people see metaphors as one type of figurative language that they might have to memorize in a poetry unit or perhaps as a big brother to a simile. But metaphors have amazing utility in all subjects; they are as natural a learning tool in science, math, physical education, music, art, and history as they are in English. Shackles off, metaphors are ready to serve any teacher of any subject in any grade level.

A map is one big metaphor. Fractal patterns are metaphors for data sets and weather patterns over time. Pine cones, a giant redwood tree, and Oreo cookies can all be metaphors for teaching. Take a look through your curriculum to see the versatility and revelation: "Water scooter" bugs skating across the stream on surface tension; verbs as the workhorses of a sentence; historical figures coming down on both sides of the same fence; a politician's remarks adding salt to the wounds; U.S. foreign policy failing to roll out the welcome mat for refugees. And, of course, "all the world's a stage."

Metaphors are most commonly processed through the mind's eye. We can understand a topic because we can see it cognitively. Marcel Danesi reminds us, "Mathematical ideas are not ingrained in the mind. They must first be imagined. It is only after they have been discovered through the power of the imagination, that they can be organized by the rational part of the mind into principles and systems of computation" (2004, 28).

If we want students to understand a topic, we have to become more adept at showing them how to picture it. The human mind thinks primarily in concrete terms, even into adulthood (Pinker 2007). Over time we become increasingly adept at translating symbolic and abstract concepts into meaningful structures or experiences. For example, when we discuss two opposing sides of an intellectual debate, we often *frame* them in terms of who is in which *corner*, suggesting a *boxing match*. When editing text, we attempt to make our language and thinking *parallel*. When describing a politician, we explain his or her *platform*.

Invention and innovation are beneficiaries of minds open to metaphorical thinking. Professor Alane Starko writes:

> Gutenberg developed the idea of movable type by looking at the way coins were stamped. Samuel Morse found the idea for relays used to transmit telegraph signals over long distances while he was traveling by stagecoach and noticing the station where horses were replaced as they began to tire. Eli Whitney said he developed the idea for the cotton gin while watching a cat trying to catch a chicken through a fence. . . . Pasteur began to understand the mechanisms of infection by seeing similarities between infected wounds and fermenting grapes. Darwin's evolutionary tree was a powerful image that was unchallenged through years of research. Einstein used moving trains to gain insight into relationships in time and space. The process of seeing or imagining how one thing might be like something else can allow new parallels to unfold, spurring hypotheses, syntheses, and perspectives. (2000, 200)

Definitions

So what exactly is a metaphor?

"Basically, metaphor is an abduction," says Zoltan Kovecses, "the result of associating certain concrete and abstract concepts to each other, not by a pure flight of fancy, but because they entail or implicate each other" (2002, 39). Interestingly, this definition uses a metaphor to describe a metaphor, which is like explaining air by referring to air. Metaphors are so unconsciously common that they become fundamental to what and how we think.

The term *metaphor* comes from the Greek *metapherein*, which means "to transfer" and "to bear" (Merriam-Webster 2004). Without much effort, we see right away how appropriate these roots are: We "transfer" or "bear" one concept/object/attribute to another, comparing something in one domain with an element in another domain. By domain, I mean the larger categories or themes into which items fit. When we describe the success of a high school play on opening night as hitting a home run, we transfer an aspect of the domain of baseball over to the domain of theater. Though many linguists use terms such as *analog, target, source, vehicle,* and *anchor* in their descriptions of metaphor, a metaphor basically reimagines or reexpresses something in one category (domain) in terms of another category (domain) to clarify or further thinking: "She is my rock." "That test was a monster." "Reading those books created my ladder of success."

Good metaphors give us *new* information (Glucksberg 2001), not the same information. They don't restate the obvious—Cars are like automobiles. To be useful, they must provide fresh perspective or insight—My son's car is a sports locker on wheels.

Many figurative language terms and rhetorical devices can be used to reexpress words and ideas. Because they assist with the transfer of abstract to concrete, we can confidently place these terms and devices under the umbrella of "metaphorical thinking." (See Appendix A for a list of metaphorical terms and devices.) This is not to say that all figurative language represents a good metaphor, only that such devices can be used to create metaphorical comparisons. For example, irony leads to metaphorical thinking when we claim that someone is as subtle as an eighteen-wheeler crashing through a tollbooth gate (metaphor: a person is a crashing eighteen-wheeler; irony: a loud, heavy, crashing truck is not usually considered subtle), or when we say an idea is as practical as a submarine with a screen door (metaphor: an idea is a dysfunctional submarine; irony: a powerful, watertight submarine would not normally include a permeable screen door). In the first example, the juxtaposition between what we expect as an example of subtlety and what really follows in the sentence—the violent crash of the truck—helps us understand the person being described. In the second example, the contrast between the impractical screen door and the underwater nature of submarines paints a picture of absurdity. The ironic statements in both instances expand our knowledge of the topic.

Almost all of us in society look for ways to reexpress our ideas, beliefs, and behaviors to ensure that others understand our meaning. For example, we can use a symbol to represent something we believe, such as when a cross is used to symbolize Christianity and a flag's markings are used to represent a country's independence. These graphic symbols visually interpret larger ideas.

Each day we are flooded with examples redescribing something in one domain in terms of another domain to clarify or advance our thinking. For example, in "Her life is a house of cards," we recognize that using playing cards to create a domicile is a fragile enterprise because the "house" frequently falls apart with the slightest breeze, nudge from our fingers, or vibration in the room. This may be similar to the chaotic relationships and economic upheaval in a person's life, each one threatening to knock the entire enterprise into disarray. You may also notice that the metaphor has become a cliché, because it is used so pervasively that it is no longer fresh to the reader. As a result, we wonder: Is this a good metaphor? It may be, if we haven't heard the cliché; more likely, we can find a better comparison that would advance our thinking. In other words, *teneo vestri celebratio*—know your audience. The skillful comparison of different terms enables us to generate the power of the metaphor, understanding its strengths and its limitations—where it doesn't work as well as where it does.

The Antimetaphor

Some of the metaphorical connections suggested here may take a little thought, but they all create the capacity to communicate a perception about one thing in terms of another. With some images, it's the antimetaphor (or negated metaphor) that actually creates the comparison and advances our insight into a topic. For example, framing the object or concept as *not* like something else forces us to consider the comparisons between two topics. Then we can sever the previous mapping points between the topics, which in turn, actually creates a clearer description of the intended topic. When referring to a man's overweight, out-of-shape body, someone might say, "Chiseled, he was not." The listener conjures the image of a man whose muscles are as defined as a sculptor's depiction of the ideal human form, and then immediately considers the opposite image of a body more flabby than refined. We've communicated one concept by denying another.

Carol Ann Tomlinson, an expert on differentiated instruction, links this antimetaphor approach to teaching. In the education world, Tomlinson says, "standards are not dinner. They are the ingredients." (Tomlinson 2008). She clarifies by reminding us that students might see a display of pepper, salt, vegetables, raw meat, bread, water, milk, butter, and other assorted foods in front of them. These are the individual standards on varied topics, but these are only the ingredients for creating a healthy meal, not the meal itself.

Dinner, or learning, involves thoughtfully assembling ingredients so that students can digest them properly and grow appropriately. We don't just lay out the spread and tell students to eat whatever and whenever they want. By declaring what academic standards are, along with what they are not, we advance our thinking about what they are.

Clarity in Metaphors

A crucial component of teaching effectively with metaphors is clarity. *New York Times* columnist William Safire emphasizes the importance of keeping metaphorical comparisons clear and simple. "Mixing the elements," he says, "especially mixing clichés, invites ridicule." Safire cites language mash-ups from the 2008 presidential election that stunned voters as well as foreign policy experts. "In the metaphor mixer, you hear examples like 'that isn't rocket surgery' and 'he's cut out of the same mold,'" Safire continues. "Rush Limbaugh once gave listeners a sinking feeling when he reportedly said, 'I knew enough to realize that the alligators were in the swamp and that it was time to circle the wagons'" (2008, 18).

Ugh. Some of us might get the gist of these comparisons because we're familiar with the clichés that are oddly linked together. Others might stumble on the meaning—or miss it entirely—because the metaphors are as clumsy as Frankenstein's monster walk. If nothing else, these examples provide good justification for teachers to fine-tune the discordant discourse through intentional and effective metaphorical instruction.

🔆 🔆 🔆

In the pages ahead, we'll explore how to teach metaphors, including physical and visual versions, as well as how to choose effective metaphors for the particular population of students we serve. We'll also examine how metaphorical thinking supports English language learners, how to create or draw upon prior knowledge so students understand the metaphors we use, and how to think critically about the limitations of metaphors. We'll further the discussion by considering how to use metaphors as assessment tools, as well as whether our current education metaphors serve to advance or limit our profession. You may want to try out the ideas in this book with a group of teachers in a professional development setting. Each chapter of the book reveals the critical role of metaphorical thinking in successful classrooms and, even better, shows teachers how to weave it into their daily activities.

2

Familiarity Breeds Content

The academic substrate in which students swim can be murky or clear to them based on their capacity to identify metaphors. If students are going to become proficient at analyzing metaphors and using them in meaningful ways, they must first develop personal metaphor "radar" that sensitizes them to the presence of metaphors. They can critique only the metaphors they can see.

In addition, whether your students are six or sixteen, they can learn to identify and use metaphors to deepen comprehension of any subject. But they—and we—need good models of metaphorical thinking. As students practice dissecting metaphors in everyday use, they discover various metaphorical forms, evaluate the effectiveness of metaphors commonly used (and overused), and start crafting their own imaginative comparisons.

Where to start? A good place to begin is focusing on something they probably already know. Take the term *brainstorm*, which teachers often encourage students to do when trying to unleash their creativity and prior knowledge about a topic. Ask students to picture the swirling ideas and chaos inside their heads as they try to brainstorm, or think of all the possible connections for a given term or topic. Explain that some of the ideas that emerge from a brainstorm won't be worth keeping, just as real storms deposit debris that we have to clean up and toss out. But during a brainstorm, we don't want to be paralyzed by correctness. The purpose is getting all the ideas out there so we can sift through them and find the treasures worth keeping.

Metaphorical Field Study

Imagine that you are anthropologist Margaret Mead quietly observing students and teachers in their natural habitat: school. You sit next to your subjects and watch them communicate. Your objective viewpoint helps you focus on previously unnoticed tools, patterns, and shortcuts. The conversations you hear are rich with metaphorical language. Though you might be outside the context of the metaphors' meanings and might not recognize each pronoun's antecedent, it's still fairly easy to catch the metaphors your subjects use readily:

- ⚡ I'm rusty on this.
- ⚡ Would this be similar to a monarchy or plutocracy?
- ⚡ We can roll with it.
- ⚡ Let's peel away the layers and see what lies in the center.
- ⚡ The cafeteria was a circus!
- ⚡ Let's bridge the two ideas.
- ⚡ Toss the idea around.
- ⚡ Let's turn that vertical thermometer horizontally to create a number line for our integers.
- ⚡ Wouldn't it be great to harness the power of the sun?
- ⚡ We're not on the same wavelength.
- ⚡ Can I grab two minutes of your time today?
- ⚡ Endoplasmic reticulum is like the circulatory system of the cell.
- ⚡ You're walking on thin ice.
- ⚡ That would require a leap of faith.

Some of these are clichés and some have become a part of conventional conversation over the years, but they were all clear to the subjects (teachers and students) using them. Like good anthropologists, we observe the communications, search for patterns, then step back to analyze the cultural significance.

This is a helpful process for students to follow as they learn to identify metaphors and their use in constructing meaning. For one activity, ask students to compile lists of analogies and metaphors they hear or read throughout the school day. They will be amazed at this unnoticed code passing between humans.

If you're working with students who have not yet learned to write or who are learning English as a second language, you can start with basic descriptions that they can layer with complexity, as a child might do by adding articles of clothing to a paper doll. Start by asking them to think about a person, a pet, or a place that resembles something else. Offer a few examples: "That cloud reminds me of a big train." "My cereal looks like a face." "My dog eats like a vacuum cleaner."

For English language learners, it might be helpful to cut out pictures of human expressions from magazines (or download them from the Internet) and match them with specific animals, such as a quiet person matched to a tree sloth, praying mantis, or sleeping cat, and an angry person connected to a charging rhinoceros or stinging bee.

Next, let students practice identifying metaphorical expressions by playing a quick classroom game. Describe something in the room in very basic terms: "The ball is round, and it is red." Or "The ball sits on top of the box." Then, continue describing the ball, but use metaphors. Whenever students hear the ball or another object being compared to something else, they can jump up and down (for younger students) or use some other mutually agreed upon signal, such as drawing a big "M" in the air with their pointer finger. Descriptions using metaphors might include: "This ball looks like a big tomato." "That ball is a whole planet to an ant." Anything that describes the ball, but is not a description of the ball's attributes, should raise their interest. For extra points or affirmation, students should identify what two things are being compared: for example, "ball and tomato" or "ball and planet earth."

Robert M. Wallace, a professor at West Virginia State University, shares an experience he had when trying to communicate metaphors to third graders:

When I asked the class, "Why do we make comparisons?" I didn't really get an answer—most were still adding to their list poems. Sharon was still writing, her small fingers wrapped around the pencil looked like a tight knot.

I should have done something to get their attention, but I just kept on talking. I didn't want to stop them. "Okay. Did you know I have a baby?"

This was the first thing that popped into my mind because I had a newborn baby at home. She had red hair just like Sharon. Maybe that's why I was focused on her; I saw my daughter in her. I folded my arms, covering my elbows with my hands, and rocked my shoulders like a cradle as I asked another question. "Now, have any of you seen my baby?"

Several kids loudly said, "No!"

"But if I tell you that my baby is as big as a football, then you know how big she is. Right?"

This time most of the class shouted, "Right!"

"So comparisons help us to understand things that we can't see. They help us to learn things." (Wallace 2005, 10–11)

Evaluating the Quality of Metaphors

It's important to show students how to evaluate the quality of metaphors in addition to recognizing and using them. (Beginners may need more practice identifying metaphors before we ask them to assess.) How do we know if metaphors are weak or strong? A metaphor may work in one context or for a particular audience, but might not be suitable in all circumstances. When does a metaphor serve its intended purpose?

To help with these evaluations, consider using the Metaphor Quality Scale provided in Figure 2.1. As you examine the criteria, keep in mind that

---

Figure 2.1 Metaphor Quality Scale

Directions:
Score one point for each attribute of the metaphor observed. Tally the points and compare the totals with the descriptions that follow. (Note, the "recipient" of the metaphor is a listener or reader to whom the metaphor is being communicated.)

___ • The items being compared can be identified by the recipient.

___ • The metaphor does not distort the truth or present false facts. (For example, planets have close-to-circular orbits around the sun, but a teacher might indicate that their path is like a rubber band. Students could interpret this comparison to mean that the orbit has a long and narrow shape. This interpretation would give a false impression of planetary pathways and thereby weaken the comparison.)

___ • When taken literally, the metaphor is false. (For example, we claim that a test is a bear, but the test is not actually a black, grizzly, brown, or polar bear. We turn the expression into a simile in our minds: "The test was very challenging, just like it would be difficult to confront a bear." For a metaphor to be strong, it can't be literally true. Otherwise, the target is just a synonym: "The canine is a dog." This example doesn't force us to transfer concepts between domains, which is the definition of a metaphor.)

___ • The items being compared exist in different domains. (For example, if the first item is a form of weather, the target comparison cannot be another form of weather: "Wow, this rainstorm is like a blizzard!" To be effective, the comparison should add to, not just restate, the recipient's understanding.)

___ • The metaphor engages the recipient personally; it's clever, insightful, and sometimes witty. (In other words, the recipient has some familiarity with the concepts being compared; a high school athlete might understand a baseball metaphor or students in an English class might grasp the comparison between a character in a novel and a character in a popular television show.)

Scale:
0–2 points: *Weak* metaphor. It's ineffective. It doesn't further or clarify thinking in a helpful way. The metaphor generates a response from the audience such as "Huh?" or "Why did the comparison repeat the topic without much thought, wasting words and time?"
3 points: *Moderately effective* metaphor. We can guess what the user intended but it requires "filling in" by the recipient. The recipient has to really think about it to understand what the user meant.
4–5 points: *Strong* metaphor. It clarifies and strengthens the recipient's understanding. It might even be clever and a model for others to follow.

---

there is no absolute way to declare metaphorical excellence; different attributes will be more or less important whenever the situation or audience changes. As you review each element with students, invite them to consider the attributes and their weighted values. Debating the merits of the weighted values would be a helpful exercise to deepen students' understanding.

Another time, ask students to spend twenty to thirty minutes sitting quietly in a public place, listening to the conversations, jotting down metaphors, and noting who is talking to whom. Back in the classroom, post and discuss the artifacts. One category might be metaphors that were overheard repeatedly. What does this suggest about the way humans communicate? Do people cement ideas in their minds by using terms over and over? Does overuse dilute or strengthen the effectiveness of a metaphor? Ask the students to recreate the scenario in which the metaphor was used, if they can recall. With those explanations, other students might be able to debate and vote on the most appropriate usage of the metaphor.

Another student conversational thread might be the way people share a common frame of reference for a metaphor. Indeed, a common frame of reference is crucial for effective communication, as we'll discuss in more detail later in the book. Without understanding the context, we can't make sense of the comparison. But when two or more people share a connection, they can speed through metaphorical thinking as fast as their synapses can fire.

To raise students' awareness and later their strategic employment of analogies and metaphors, give them multiple "critical eye" experiences (both verbal and written), in which they have to identify the analogies and metaphors used. "Working with a partner, find ten or more metaphors on this page of text," should be a frequent prompt, as well as, "Who can find a metaphor in this magazine advertisement?" and, "Find a metaphor in one e-mail or text message received this week."

As students analyze metaphors in everyday use, ask them to first identify the item and then explain what it means in the context given. Here's an example:

> **Metaphor:** "Google it."
> **Definition:** Google is a popular Internet search engine. Instead of the longer statement, "Go to the Internet, find a search engine, and look for the topic using that search engine," people shorten it to something that represents that whole process—the name of a common search engine, Google. Because "Google" has no commonly understood definition other than as the search engine, it's useful in this context. While it's similar to the math term, *googol*, which is a one followed by 100 zeroes, the homonyms are not spelled the same. The context and spelling keep the listener referring to the metaphor intended by the speaker.

Choose short snippets of dialogue or text examples, because they will help students focus and build identification skills quickly. Use multiple formats whenever possible, so students will understand how widespread metaphors are. Consider news articles, textbook pages, directions, text messages, advertisements, political speeches, teachers' lectures, wikis, cartoons, blogs, and newscasts, among others.

Basic Building Blocks

Before they can accurately identify and assess metaphors, students have to know what they're looking for. How young is too young to grasp the concept? At an elementary level, young children can see metaphor as a form of "pretend" comparison. They imagine that their crayons are tiny swords and use them to reenact a battle scene on top of their desks. The metaphorical crayon substitutes for the real sword.

As children mature, teachers can broaden the scope of their metaphorical vision. Here's a sample conversation from a first-grade class:

Teacher: Hannah just said we were flying through these pictures. What does that mean? Are we really flying with our wings out like birds?

Tina: No.

Teacher: Then what did she mean?

Gabe: That we're going fast.

Teacher: Is that what birds do when they fly—go fast?

(Class nods.)

Evan: But sometimes they go slow when there's a wind.

Teacher: I go slowly when there's a strong wind, too. It's hard to walk. *(Teacher smiles.)* What Gabe said was another meaning for "flying," however, and it was accurate. Can we fly through our breakfast?

(Students giggle.)

Teacher: *(Pretends to eat breakfast very quickly.)* Am I flying through my breakfast?

(Students nod, smiling.)

Teacher: *(Pretends to eat slowly.)* Am I flying through my breakfast?

(Class shakes head no.)

Teacher: So, sometimes, we use words we know mean one thing to describe other things, too. Is there anything else we can fly through like this?

Micah: We can fly through a circle.

Teacher: Yes, we can, if it was big enough, and that would be fun wouldn't it? We can fly through anything with a hole big enough as long as we had big wings . . .

Micah: *(Interrupting.)* . . . Or a rocket pack!

Jennifer: Or just magic, too.

Teacher: *(Nodding.)* When we were flying through the set of pictures earlier, we were not going through something. *(Pantomimes with her forearm going through a larger hole formed by her other arm curved into a pretend hole.)* We were going fast. When we were talking about flying through breakfast, we were talking about eating breakfast quickly. So here, flying is not about lifting up into the air. It's about doing something quickly. Can anyone pantomime "flying" like this through coloring a picture?

(Students nod and pantomime quickly scribbling a picture and turning it in to the teacher.)

Teacher: *(Laughing.)* Yes, that's right. Boy, these would be very messy pictures, wouldn't they? They might even be strange colors and in strange shapes!

Terrell: I can fly through my piano lesson.

Teacher: I bet. You have fast fingers. *(Pantomimes playing the piano.)* Is there anything we don't want to fly through because we like it so much we want it to last longer?

Carolyn: My birthday party. It's next week. Do you know that I went to a cave?

Teacher: For your birthday?

Carolyn: No, when we were visiting my grandma. She lives near Carlsbad.

Teacher: *(Gesturing with a quick hand swish in the air.)* Did you "fly" quickly through your visit to the cave, or did you *(slowing the gesture down)* take your time to see everything?

Carolyn: We walked slowly. It was dark. We could hit our heads, and there was lots of bat poop.

Teacher: Wow, you don't want to "fly" through a dark cave do you? You might hit your head and step in poop! Join me now, class. *(Passes one palm across the other palm in a quick, elongated gesture.)* This is flying through something quickly, and *(slowly passing one palm across the other without the elongated gesture)* this is doing it slowly. Practice with me.

(Teacher and students practice motions and statement of each motion.)

Teacher: Now, each of you tell me one thing that it's okay to fly through quickly and make the correct motion as you do.

(Students give examples, and teacher models with the class as they do the motions.)

Teacher: Now let's do the hand motions for things we don't want to fly through quickly.

(Students give examples, and teacher models with the class the slower motion.)

Teacher: Great!

Micah: Can we please not fly through music today?

Teacher: I like the way you think, Micah.

Young students understand metaphor. Peggy Parish's Amelia Bedelia series is a good resource for exploring humorous comparisons and explaining idioms to children and English language learners. The main character, a literal-minded housekeeper, puts real sponges into her sponge cake recipe, replants dandelions and violets as she weeds her garden, and sprinkles powder in the living room when she dusts the furniture. And when she pitches a tent, she throws it into the woods.

Going on a Treasure Hunt

Routinely identifying metaphors in our conversations and lessons prepares students to find and analyze metaphors on their own. Older students need practice as much as young children do. Because metaphors are so ubiquitous, they are easy to overlook. Encouraging students to examine relationships between terms and objects in both written and spoken language gives them a firm foothold for metaphorical explorations.

Let's keep substitutions, comparisons, and re-representations in front of students:

- ⚡ "The Police Officer is our friend. What do friends do that is like what Police Officers do?"
- ⚡ "This doesn't make sense. I'm confused. I feel like my brain is walking through thick mud. What do you think I need to do to get back up to speed?"
- ⚡ "The economy this week is behaving like it's surfing the Banzai Pipeline on Oahu's north shore in Hawaii. What are the characteristics of the current economy that are similar to what surfers on the Pipeline experience?

Repeated moments of identifying the comparisons used in our conversations and lessons help prepare students to identify and analyze metaphors on their own. Make it a group game, if possible, charting as many samples of metaphorical thinking and comparisons as students can find in one day or week of school. Older students also will need continued practice with identifying metaphors and analogies in use. Some expressions are so embedded in our daily lives that they will be hard to catch as metaphors in the moment: "Who penned the paper?" "Do you grasp this?" "That photo really pops."

Initially students may be confused by a comparative reference, either because the analogy or metaphor is unfamiliar or because they don't understand the vocabulary. For example, students who are unsure what the term *rhetoric* means in the question, "Did he use the same rhetoric as his predecessors?" will not know whether the confusion stems from an unclear metaphor or an unknown definition for rhetoric.

To help students know when an analogy or metaphor is being used, teach them the following strategies. First, they can search for language clues that indicate comparisons. These terms may include "such as," "like," "similar to," "[subject] is [subject]," as well as figurative language or thinking: personification, allegory, parables, simile, colloquialism, and metaphor. Second, they can look up the definition of the unknown vocabulary or ask about the meaning of the word. If the definition doesn't literally match the word's use in the sentence, they may have stumbled upon another interpretation or culturally based reference—maybe a metaphor. Finally, if the author is trying to describe something by comparing it to something else, that's a clue that the mysterious word or phrase could be a metaphor, because metaphors are often used for ideas that are otherwise hard to explain.

Push Students to Examine the Metaphor

After we have given students time to practice identifying and using metaphors and analogies, we want to extend their thinking about the comparisons. Kelly Gallagher's excellent book, *Deeper Reading*, describes many ways that teachers can use metaphors to guide students' meaning making, particularly in understanding literature. I've adapted some questions that Gallagher (2004, 131) uses to jumpstart students' meta-cognitive inquiries:

⚡ Why did the author use a particular metaphor or analogy and not one slightly different? Provide students with a few alternatives. For example, "Instead of comparing it to an oak tree, why didn't he use a pine tree or a rose

Rhetoric presents an interesting case for metaphor archeologists. Rhetoric refers to the language, content, and reasoning woven together to persuade listeners and readers of a particular point of view (ideology). Rhetoric often incorporates specific metaphors to make a case, and the best metaphors typically solidify arguments and sway opinions.

Interacting with rhetoric, in particular competing ideals, is one way we create knowledge in our society. Exposure to rhetoric can also help students recognize bias and inspire independent thinking: With his new funding proposal, did the politician *pave* the way for community improvements (lay down a clear, easier path), bulldoze over his constituents' wishes (deny their wishes and push his own agenda), or both? American political parties use rhetoric to their advantage, but so do lawyers, judges, school boards, pharmaceutical companies, sports teams, textbook publishers, bloggers, and movie producers. Knowing how to deconstruct rhetoric is a valuable tool for citizens.

Let's go to the history books for an example of rhetoric in debate. During the Scopes trial in Tennessee during the 1920s, for instance, the prosecution facetiously jabbed at evolutionists by bringing caged chimpanzees into town as witnesses for the defense. Defense attorney Clarence Darrow said that the prosecution was "opening the doors for a reign of bigotry equal to anything in the Middle Ages." Darrow also said that the prosecution's argument meant that the Bible was the only "yardstick to measure every man's intellect, to measure every man's intelligence, to measure every man's learning" (Linder 2008). This made a point without denouncing belief in the Bible, which was a good rhetorical move by Darrow as he was trying to persuade Fundamentalists, not alienate them.

Rhetoric could refer to a general definition of the term (a synonym and, thus, not a metaphor) or to the collective discourse and associated acts of previous political leaders, which would lead to comparisons of ideology—a metaphor. Straddling denotative and connotative worlds, rhetoric can build a bridge of understanding when students are starting out on the metaphorical journey.

bush?" or "Instead of comparing it to an ant hill, why didn't he compare it to a bee hive or a rattlesnake's nest?"

⚡ How can the metaphor or analogy be improved? Continuing the evolution theme discussed in the Scopes trial, for example, students might be inclined initially to portray human evolution as a tall, tri-angular object, like the Eiffel Tower, with human presence on top. This image is similar to that in Mark Twain's observation: "If the Eiffel Tower were now representing the world's age, the skin of paint on the pinnacle-knob at its summit would represent man's share of that age; & anybody would perceive that that skin was what the tower was built for" (Twain 1903). Not everyone grasps this one immediately, but it's a powerful conceit for evolutionary perspective.

Students considering this metaphor in light of current knowl-edge of evolutionary paths quickly realize that large branches of flora and fauna break away from a uniform ascent, unlike the shape of the Eiffel Tower. A better portrayal of branching evolution, stu-dents might surmise, would be to reimagine evolution as multiple ascending structures of varying sizes growing out of a common cir-cumference. Hey, that might look like a Saguaro cactus. So they decide that a Saguaro cactus makes a better metaphor here.

⚡ Does the metaphor or analogy break down at some point? Metaphors can break down if the wrong ones are generated uninten-tionally by students, and they can break down if they can't hold up to the full comparison done by students. For example, describing someone who is light in weight as "skating on thin ice" doesn't work very well; if he or she is so light, there is little danger of ice breaking. This is another call for vigilant, formative assessment to check for understanding.

⚡ Why did the author use a metaphor or analogy? What was he or she trying to convey? (Or, conversely, why *didn't* the author use a metaphor or analogy at this point? Would a strong comparison have helped?)

⚡ Could the author have used some other rhetorical or language device to communicate this same concept just as clearly? If so, what would also work here?

⚡ What makes a metaphor or analogy effective for the reader/listener/viewer?

⚡ Is this metaphor or analogy effective, or not? Why?

Gallagher writes: "Teaching students to think metaphorically helps them to appreciate the richness and liveliness of language. Thinking this way sharpens their interpretative skills and helps them reach deeper understanding. . . . Being able to interpret metaphors in a novel means that students will be able to interpret metaphors in a politician's speech, or in an advertisement, or in a favorite song. In this way students are taught critical thinking skills that stay with them long after they have read the last book of the school year" (2004, 145).

See Chapter 9 for more ideas on how to get students to examine the limitations of metaphors and analogies.

With and Without Metaphors

Another activity to sow the seeds of metaphorical thinking asks students to explain an abstract or complex topic in detail without using comparative language or descriptions. This assignment reinforces the ubiquity and utility of metaphors in our lives; they are as important as legs are for walking.

You may want to focus on an academic (school-related) topic or concept, but remain open to personal interests as well. Choose a topic that will require students to emphasize the "what," not the "how," of the thing. For example, it's far easier to tell someone how to make a sandwich, change a tire, or fling a Frisbee, because sequential steps and physical elements are involved. Conversely, abstractions almost require comparisons; if we don't know what "it" is, we must search for similarities to guide our mental recognition. Here are some abstract topics for exploration:

Friendship	Family
Infinity	Imperialism
Solving for a variable	Trust
Euphoria	Mercy
Worry	Trouble
Obstructionist judiciary	Honor
Immigration	Homeostasis
Balance	Temporal rifts
Economic principles	Religious fervor
Poetic license	Semantics
Heuristics	Tautology
Embarrassment	Knowledge

Students' descriptions should include detailed definitions of the term, using metaphorical language, followed by detailed descriptions that do not use metaphorical language. Sonia, a student in Moosa Shah's seventh-grade science class at Rachel Carson Middle School in Herndon, Virginia, provides a good example of this process when using metaphors to describe experimental design:

> An experimental design is like an owner's manual. It tells you what to do, when to do it, and how to do it. Everything is already carefully planned out and edited. All you have to do is read it and go from step 1 to step 2.

Later, she was asked to describe experimental design without using any comparative language. Her response:

> Experimental design is the design of all information-gathering exercises where variation is present, whether under the full control of the experimenter or not. The experimenter is often interested in the effect of some process or intervention on some objects which may be people.

Chris, another student in Shah's class, described one portion of mitosis using metaphorical language:

> Then the centrioles pull the parts of the chromosomes apart like a game of tug of war. Then cytokinesis occurs and splits the cell with a pinch-like way or by forming a cell plate within the cell.

When asked to describe the same phenomenon without using metaphors, he wrote:

> Mitosis is the process when a eukaryotic cell separates the chromosomes in its nucleus into two identical daughter nuclei. It is usually formed by the process of cytokinesis.

Two students tackled photosynthesis. Here is Emily's take on one aspect of the process using metaphors to explain:

> Photosynthesis is similar to our solar panels. Both use the sun's energy (or light) to make energy . . . As photosynthesis is to plant energy, solar panels are to electricity! . . . Inside the plant cells is where the whole process starts, in chloroplasts. They turn CO_2, light energy, and water into glucose (sugars) and oxygen, like an input-output machine.

Here is Emily's explanation without using metaphors:

> Photosynthesis uses energy from light and simple compounds to make sugar, which is full of energy. This starts when the plant takes in water and CO_2 from the environment. With this, the plant will produce energy-rich carbon compounds, as well as oxygen.

Continuing the theme, Rohan wrote about photosynthesis using metaphors:

> One can think of the chloroplasts as miniature farms for the plants. After all, they are organelles that produce a great amount of the energy for the organism itself, and the food that they produce sustains the local leaf and the organism itself, just as a farm would be able to sustain the local town. . . . Without the process of photosynthesis, plants would die from a lack of nutrients, which would set off a chain reaction, causing most animals, including upper-level predators and consumers, to become extinct. Think of the consequences as a row of dominoes. Once you trip the first one, they all surrender, one after another, and none are standing when the final domino has fallen.

Here is Rohan's description without metaphors:

> This occurs in the unique, green organelles known as chloroplasts, found only in autotrophs . . . Water and carbon dioxide, along with sunlight, are processed in the chloroplasts. . . . If photosynthesis were to stop, both animals and plants would be facing utter extinction.

Finally, Mr. Shah's student Lily wrote about eutrophication using metaphors:

> The excessive growth is called an "algal bloom" since algae often grow quickly and plentifully as a result. Eutrophication can cause other organisms to die, since extra algae use up resources that the plants already there would normally use. This is similar to the overcrowding of a building, with people competing for space and resources.

And here is Lily's explanation without using metaphors:

> The nutrients stimulate plant growth, or algal blooms, where many plants such as algae grow in vast amounts. The algae can use up resources in the water, harming other plants.

There are a couple of things to notice in these examples: First, while students try their best, some metaphorical thinking sneaks into the descriptions supposedly devoid of metaphors. It's hard to describe something without using metaphors. Second, and more important, notice how much richer the descriptions are *with* metaphors. While the nonmetaphor descriptions may have taken some thought, they are little more than echoes from a textbook, lecture, Web site, or informational video. They represent passive learning that has little chance of surviving the school year. The "metaphor'd" descriptions, however, require more engagement on the part of students. As a result, we immediately know what students truly understand about the topic and whether they will retain the information longer. Generating metaphors is akin to teaching the concept to others, one of the highest forms of knowledge.

3

Archimedes' Metaphorical Legacy: The Right Tools for the Job

"Give me a place to stand on, and I will move the earth," said Archimedes, the Greek inventor, astronomer, physicist, and mathematician. He proved the point in many disciplines, discovering new mathematical and scientific principles as well as designing dozens of new machines, including engines and screws still used today. His legacy applies to our study of metaphors: Given the right tools, our students can construct, apply, and extend metaphorical thinking in amazing ways.

The strategies are not just for students. As teachers, we can benefit from the same tools we share with students, using metaphors to design lessons, conduct classes, assess understanding, and reflect professionally. Throughout this book, ask yourself: How can I use the recommended strategy to improve my own metaphor construction? Could I also use this strategy to assess students' mastery of the topic?

Let's step back now to identify the planning sequence that we can follow when choosing and/or building our own metaphors and analogies. Then we'll consider how to use these same tools for assessment.

Choosing the Right Metaphor

Choose any topic you have to teach: chromatic scale, electromagnetism, ancient Egypt, tariffs, constitutional law, peristalsis, enzymes, colonization, wash your hands before eating, the role of the police department in our community, *Artemis Fowl*, four-quadrant graphing, the Industrial Revolution, hypertext, figurative language, Boolean logic, liquid and dry measure, sine and cosine, conflict resolution, cursive writing—any topic specific to your curriculum. Whatever the topic, the first step is breaking it down. What are its basic components?

When adding fractions, for example, we need to know about greatest common factor, least common multiple, numerator, denominator, mixed numbers, reducing to lowest terms, common denominator, part-of-a-whole, and more. When teaching an essay's theme, we'd identify the definition of theme, message, the theme's interwoven nature, supporting details, claims, and author's intent, among other ideas. List all of the components you can think of. Doing this will spark both larger and smaller metaphor and analogy ideas.

Second, choose comparisons that are relevant to students. Instead of a purely symbolic chemistry problem about recombinations of atoms and molecules using chemical equations, we may substitute students' experiences at the recent homecoming dance for the corresponding factors in the equation. For younger students learning about taxation without representation, we could ask them how they would feel if someone forced them to pay for skateboards (or Razor scooters), but wouldn't let them choose where, when, or if they could use them. The goal is to make abstract ideas as concrete and personally affecting as possible.

If you can't identify a connection to students' lives, you may want to consider creating a common frame of reference (the base or source of our metaphor) to which you can connect the target: the topic you're trying to teach. For example, if you're about to teach about the rise of the Ottoman Empire after the conquest of Constantinople and you're going to use J.R.R. Tolkien's epic story, *The Lord of the Rings*, as a frame of reference, you'll have to acquaint students with the basic story line, including the attacks on Saruman in Isengard, the armies of Rohan and Aragon, the armies of Sauron, and the battles of Minas Tirith in Gondor. If you're going to use the board game Risk instead, you'll have to familiarize students with the game's format.

Remember that some metaphors and analogies can raise deep and troubling sentiments among our diverse students. The Ottomans ruled over much of the Muslim world at one point, including southwest Asia and northern Africa. An attempt to compare something very complex and emotional to a simplistic role-playing game or a classic trilogy depicting good versus evil may offend some students, particularly Muslim students in this case. Before launching into such comparisons, it's wise to seek the perspective of colleagues, and even students' families.

Third, "test drive" the metaphor or analogy with others whose opinions you trust. You might be so close to a topic that you lack an objective view that would enable you to see weak spots in the metaphor's application. "Just saying it aloud to yourself, let alone others, really helps," says Reverend Tom Berlin, pastor of Floris United Methodist Church in Herndon, Virginia. This process forces you to put your thoughts in order, directing the listener toward your ultimate message, the comparison. Reverend Berlin adds, "Make sure the person with whom you share your story can identify the metaphor and message on his own."

Fourth, double-check that the metaphor or analogy furthers your cause. Does it really reveal or reinforce substantive information regarding your topic? Or does it represent a "fluff" moment in the lesson that threatens momentum, becoming more distracting than instructive?

Along these same lines, play the devil's advocate and run through every imaginable misinterpretation students might develop as a result of the comparisons. Could students get the wrong idea about the topic if we use this metaphor? If they hold on to this one too strongly, will it prevent them from learning about the exceptions, nuances, and subtleties later? If so, how could we reframe the comparison so this doesn't happen? Do we need to use some smaller comparisons earlier in the lesson?

Consider all the what-if's: What if students say . . .? What if they ask about . . .? What if this doesn't clarify things for them? Try to imagine each worst-case scenario and create a thoughtful response. Considering the limitations of the metaphor not only helps us decide whether to use it, but also helps us adjust instruction if misconceptions occur as a result. Guiding prompts might include: "Some of you might be thinking that . . .," "As we look at this, be careful not to equate . . .," "In this comparison, you might conclude . . . but that is not entirely correct, because . . ."

Finally, encourage students to reflect on the usefulness of metaphors from our lessons. Did the comparison help them understand something more clearly? How would they change or improve it for the next time you teach this lesson? Can they think of a better metaphor?

Despite prudent thinking and preparation, you may use incorrect or offensive metaphors in class from time to time. If so, use the imperfection as a teachable moment. Suppose a metaphor offends a student because it oversimplifies history or discounts the emotions of a political or ethnic group. Metaphors are often flawed or limited, and a discussion would uncover the blemishes. Readers may remember the trouble that President George W. Bush got into when he referred to the United States' invasion of Iraq as a "crusade." His metaphor revealed his ignorance of or disregard for

Figure 3.1 Planning Sequence for Generating Metaphors and Analogies for Instructional Use

1. Break the topic into its component pieces.
2. Identify comparisons with the topic that are relevant to students' lives, making abstract ideas as concrete and personally affecting as possible. Create a common frame of reference in students if necessary.
3. "Test drive" the metaphor or analogy with others whose opinions you trust. Make sure the person can identify the metaphor and message on his own.
4. Double-check that the metaphor or analogy furthers your cause, won't confuse students, and actually adds to instruction instead of weakens it. Adjust the comparisons as necessary to maximize their effect.
5. After using a metaphor or analogy, ask students to evaluate its helpfulness.

a historical term that is loaded with baggage for Muslims, both moderates and extremists.

Or consider how some historians have written about America's westward expansion as a "manifest destiny" to civilize native tribes and take what they perceived to be theirs. In historical context, *civilize* was code for bringing Christianity to the indigenous and eliminating their traditions. Native children were sent to Indian schools, where their long hair was cut, their native dress was exchanged for that of whites, and so forth. The children were beaten if they spoke their original languages. All human societies, not just Eurocentric ones, are civilizations. In the context of manifest destiny, the term *civilize* took on a much more insidious tone. The goal was to eliminate social variations—one group's manifest destiny was another culture's annihilation. The point is that as a teacher you will occasionally step on someone's toes. Apologize, examine the bruises, educate yourself, and then move on with more insight and surer footing.

Figure 3.1 includes the abbreviated outline of the recommended planning sequence.

Metaphors and Analogies as Assessment Tools

When students create their own metaphors regarding content, they reveal what they understand about that content, often in a manner that expresses their level of proficiency more clearly than they could through other forms of assessment. Metaphor making as assessment can provide amazing insight.

Consider for a moment what evidence you and your colleagues will accept as evidence of student mastery, understanding, or proficiency in an area of study. For example, when it comes to xylem and phloem (vascular transport structures for plants), what level of understanding meets the standard of excellence or learner outcomes set for these topics in your department or grade level? When students are writing introductions to essays, what represents excellent, just getting by, or not even close to competent? Now consider whether a student-constructed metaphor or analogy could provide acceptable evidence of learning.

In many cases, the metaphors will be effective, although they might reveal different aspects of students' understanding than you anticipated. If you're assessing whether students can write an expository paragraph, you will need to ask more of them than simply creating a metaphor or an analogy to explain expository paragraph writing. They must actually write an expository paragraph; waxing metaphorical doesn't cut it when we need the tangible product. However, if we want to know if students recognize the larger structure or big picture of expository paragraph writing, a metaphor or analogy could demonstrate their understanding. Their chosen metaphors or analogies would reveal their sense of the big picture and that, in turn, can also expose faulty reasoning that we can correct with targeted instruction.

Consider, too, the powerful formative assessment nature of metaphors and analogies. Formative assessments are assigned during the course of learning, not at the end of learning. The data from these assessments should guide instructional decisions and provide specific feedback to students in a timely and useful manner so that they can revise their thinking and deepen skills before attempting the assessment again. And then we must ensure that they get the opportunity for reassessment. Through revising, students learn about themselves as well as gain new strategies for learning.

Formative assessment supports learning standards or outcomes. In my own classes over the years, I noticed that students who repeatedly struggled to learn what I was teaching usually didn't know where they stood in relation to the lesson's goals. Successful students were much more likely to know the purpose and how close they were to meeting the objectives. Frequent formative assessment provides this awareness. When I helped struggling students see their progress each week, their motivation and learning improved.*

When students generate their own metaphors and analogies as a formative assessment, we see what they "map" from one concept to another; we become aware of connections made and not made and learning that occurred or did not occur. Generating analogies reveals misconceptions in ways that

---

*Paul Black and Dylan William concluded that formative assessment is key to successful teaching, no matter the subject. In *Inside the Black Box: Raising Standards through Classroom Assessment* (1989), Black and William also make the case that frequent formative assessment improves students' learning, with the greatest gains coming from academically struggling students.

simply answering recall questions does not, especially when we ask students to elaborate on their "mapping" strategies. When we push students to defend their thinking—"Where does the metaphor or analogy break down in the comparison? Can you improve the metaphor or analogy in some way? Is the metaphor or analogy effective or ineffective, and why do you believe as you do?"—we gain insights about how well students understand concepts. In turn, this information can help us plan and adapt our instruction.

Given the science class prompt, "Define the terms *rotation* and *revolution*," students might memorize a dictionary or teacher definition, but they do not have to think critically about the concepts or move the knowledge into long-term memory. In addition, the answers don't tell us whether they can apply their knowledge.

What if we changed the prompt to reflect metaphorical thinking?

Compare the concepts of rotation and revolution to a favorite sport or to society in general. Demonstrate the comparisons by clearly mapping the characteristics of each concept. Once you've shown the appropriate correlation, identify one misconcept about each concept, rotation and revolution, which classmates might develop if your metaphor or analogy was the only thing they knew about each concept. In other words, identify one limitation for each of your comparisons.

Students will respond to this prompt in different ways. Their first step, however, will be to carefully define both *rotation* and *revolution* as related to the science field for themselves. The definitions will be similar to the following:

Rotation: an object moving in a circular motion around a center point or axis, and if the axis is within the object itself, the rotation is called "spin."
Revolution: an object in a circular motion around an external point, such as the moon revolving around the earth. In some cases, however, revolution can be used as a synonym for rotation.

Once they have defined the terms, students should demonstrate the characteristics of rotation and revolution in a chosen sport or aspect of society. There are ample sports connections here for rotation: In tennis, players slice the air with their rackets as they connect with the ball to create topspin and backspin on the ball. A baseball pitcher changes his finger position to create enough spin to curve the ball's trajectory just before it reaches the batter. We can create a similar effect when releasing a bowling ball toward the pins. A spiral pass thrown by a quarterback in American football has a horizontal spin axis. In each sports moment, the ball spins around an internal axis to affect an intended outcome.

In her test response, one student wonders about the command to "rotate" when switching positions in a volleyball game. The players seem more to revolve around a point external to themselves. She asks, isn't this a "revolution"? Why do they call it "rotation" instead? The student ponders further, questioning the auto mechanic's recommendation to rotate the tires on a car so the tread will wear evenly. It would seem that the tires are revolving around the car's chassis, not turning around an internal axis. "They do that [rotate] when they actually roll on the road," the student thinks. She realizes that factories rotate inventory and a revolving door at a hotel actually rotates around a central axis—is that a rotation, too? Maybe all of this is okay, the student concludes, because rotation and revolution are synonymous in some contexts. Questioning the use of the terms enables the student to apply knowledge in various situations.

The prompt also allows students to choose an application to society. Here she claims that some authors revolve around breakthrough authors. For example, after Dan Brown's *The Da Vinci Code* became an international best seller, publishers scrambled to produce similar archeological thrillers. The market was flooded with historical tales of mystery, many related to the Catholic Church, the focus of Brown's work. Some of the newer books have elevated the genre—achieving escape velocity from *The Da Vinci Code*'s shadow, much as a satellite revolving around Earth would do with enough thrust.

The continued metaphor holds in other aspects of society as well: The early colonists for the United States could be said to have created enough critical mass (literally and politically) and momentum to achieve "escape velocity" from England and the Church. What enables a sub-group within society to achieve such mass and forward momentum, or for the majority society to let the sub-group choose a separate path?

Another student makes the case that the world is rallying around "green" technology, the fight against global warming, and the eradication of AIDS. Time, energy, and people flow round the focus topic, just as planets do around the sun. The student sees little impact from the United States government's repetitive practice of using tax breaks to stimulate the economy, and suggests that the country is "spinning" in place. But the student also realizes that while spinning, the United States also continues along its path—the political and cultural orbital revolution through life, just as the earth spins or rotates while continuing along its orbital path, revolving around the sun.

Using Johannes Kepler's discovery that planets revolve in elliptical, not circular, orbits, advanced students might consider what elements in our society may be at apogee (farthest point from the center object) and perigee (closest point to the center object). For instance, we may rally legally and politically around our constitution, but is our thinking far or close to a constitutional focus? The Supreme Court helps us interpret that spatial relationship every session. And, just as early discoverers debated geocentric versus heliocentric orbits, the focus object of our current societal revolutions color everything we do: Is our economy service-based? Are we technocentric? What reference do we use to establish social morality—the Bible? The Koran? Secularism? How does our focus object affect our orbital revolution?

The second version of the prompt encourages critical thinking about the terms *rotation* and *revolution*. Each step provides opportunities for teachers to see how students' thinking holds up or falls apart, and to step in and help as necessary. With this information, we can provide helpful feedback and revise our instruction—two primary goals of formative assessment.

The rotation/revolution comparison targets students at the secondary level or beyond. But if you teach lower grade levels, you can reach for sophisticated connections as well, using language your students would understand. I've had success with the rotation/revolution prompt with both younger and older students, though I changed the wording. Metaphorical thinking is innate in humans. First-grade students *can* think this way. We just have to get them comfortable with the process.

Consider the learning continuum as well. Novices think of new ideas or information as individual items. They don't see patterns or relationships. They make limited connections and have little context to build understanding. It's no wonder that they have trouble remembering all the random and seemingly isolated data they encounter in a typical day. Metaphorical thinking helps students start chunking information, attaching individual ideas to others in their minds as if they were fitting puzzle pieces together on a table top. Teachers can lead students to these discoveries through intentional instruction that builds meaning through effective comparisons. That's how we move novice learners to expert status.

When looking at the assessment applications of metaphors and analogies, start with your objectives. If your objective is to determine if students can follow the specific sequence of a math algorithm, asking them to think metaphorically may not be appropriate. But if you want to find out if students have learned how isolated concepts fit within the larger picture of mathematical theory and applications, you could ask them to draw analogies or express their ideas metaphorically. If you want to see if they can explain complex ideas in any subject, the metaphors and analogies reveal very specific levels of understanding. As a result, you get a better picture of their proficiency with each unit or lesson.

Now that we've planted the seeds of effective lesson planning and assessment incorporating metaphorical thinking, let's make sure to cultivate these frameworks as we work with the specific strategies in the chapters that follow.

Walking in Our Students' Shoes, and Sometimes Making the Shoes Ourselves

Pretend that you are a student and your teacher has just asked you to access a Web site where he has collected resources about a topic. At the Web site, you are directed to a page link, which contains a poem that you must read and a series of questions that you must answer. Here are the poem and questions:

> Worthy they were,
> Rafael, Leonardo, Michelangelo, and Donatello.
> Their's a chromatic and plumed rebirth,
> A daring reflection upon man.
> Beyond Hastings and a Wife's tale in Canterbury,
> Galileo thrust at more than Windmills,
> He, Copernicus Gravitas.
> And for the spectre of debate,
> religion blinked then jailed,
> errant no more,
> thereby errant forever.
> Cousin to Pericles, Son of Alexander,
> The cosmology of Adam fanned for all,
> feudal plains trampled by trumpeters,
> man and woman lay awake—

calves on wobbly legs,
staring at new freedom
and Gutenberg's promise.

1. What's the main topic of the poem, and how do you know?
2. Why did the poet call the works of the first four people *chromatic* and *plumed*?
3. How was their rebirth a daring reflection upon man?
4. Why was Galileo's quest said to be thrusting at windmills?
5. What was the debate about his discoveries?
6. Why did the church blink, and how could it be errant no more and at the same time be errant forever?
7. Who or what was cousin to Pericles and son of Alexander, and how is it related to these two historical figures?
8. Why would man and woman be considered calves on wobbly legs?
9. What was Gutenberg's promise?
10. What was the poet's intent, and did she or he achieve it?

For some students, the poem and the follow-up questions would be as meaningless as a blob of ink on a page. They have no guide to translation. A few students might see the names Rafael, Leonardo, Michelangelo, and Donatello and incorrectly connect them to the comic book heroes the Teenage Mutant Ninja Turtles instead of to the Renaissance artists the poet (in this case, me) intended. Copernicus Gravitas? Hmm. Maybe he was an evil villain.

By contrast, students who know the background of the Renaissance period in history will understand that the poem provides repeated commentary on the tone of the era as well as the cultural, scientific, and artistic transformations it generated. Armed with this knowledge, students can easily answer the comprehension questions and use the poem as fodder for further discussion about the church's role in shaping society.

Calling upon this familiarity as they learn new information is critical to students' success. In fact, it's in the top nine all-time best teaching strategies (Marzano 2001). Without the right background knowledge, students will drift off, in this case dreaming of turtles and villains. To move them from daydreams to real-time learning, we may have to create cerebral context where there is none.

Let's see how this process plays out in the classroom. For just a moment, consider Gerald in his fifth-period science class. The teacher explains that shifting tides in the Atlantic Ocean move like water in the bathtub when the bather moves from one side to the other: As the water rises on one side of the tub, it lowers on the other, then it sloshes back to the other side and does this several times before settling. The teacher then says that low tide on the east coast of the United States would be high tide on the west coast of Africa, and vice versa, due to the gravitational pull of both the sun and moon. The basin holding the Atlantic Ocean is the bathtub.

Gerald comes from a family that doesn't take baths. They use showers instead. Though Gerald might create an image in his mind's eye of how shifting tides are like shifting water in a bathtub, it has little meaning for him. The metaphor doesn't help him move the knowledge into long-term memory as a result. He tolerates the teacher's comparison more than he assimilates it.

As Gerald's teacher notices this lack of engagement or confusion in her student, she has to make a choice: move on to the next point without clarifying anything for Gerald (*He'll understand it better in the lab we're doing today*, the teacher reasons), draw a picture and explain the metaphor in more detail, or choose a more relevant metaphor based on what she knows about Gerald. Each of these three alternatives can be appropriate, depending on the situation, but in this case the teacher thinks it's worth coming up with a more meaningful metaphor. Because she thought she might need to use it during the lesson, she pulls out a prop she had prepared earlier: a large plastic bowl filled half way with colored water. She holds it low enough so Gerald can see inside the bowl, then she slowly tips it to the left. As she tips it, the water level on the right side seems to lower down the side of the bowl as the water on the left rises.

"That's what happens on Earth?" Gerald asks. "The earth tilts while the water stays level? The land rises above the water?"

Oh my, the teacher thinks. *That's not what I wanted him to notice at all. This is the wrong metaphor.* She searches her mind for what she knows about Gerald. Some time ago, she realizes, she learned that Gerald's family has several children and extended family members living together in a two-bedroom apartment. She hits on a connection:

"Gerald, imagine sharing a bed with someone else because there are not enough sleeping places for everyone to have his or her own bed." She phrases it this way so it doesn't call attention to his family's daily financial stress. Gerald nods.

"What does the person on the left side of the bed do with the blanket when he rolls over to his side of the bed?" the teacher asks.

"He pulls it with him," Gerald replies.

"Right. And what happens to the person on the other side of the bed when the person on the left pulls the blanket over on himself?"

"He gets cold," Gerald replies.

"Right again," the teacher says. "So there's only so much blanket. When it's pulled to the left side of the bed, there's less of it covering the person on the right side. The same thing happens when the person on the right pulls the blanket back to his side of the bed. It's now off you and you get cold."

"Yeah, it can be a tug of war," Gerald replies.

"So how is this connected to the shifting tides?"

"You're saying something's pulling the ocean to each side?" Gerald asks.

"Yes," says the teacher. "The moon and sun's gravities. With the tides, it's one big blanket tug of war."

We try to use metaphors connected with students' backgrounds, but this isn't always possible, especially when working with diverse populations. Even in a relatively homogeneous community there are differences significant enough to warrant creating a common frame of reference. Our students read different books, mature at different rates, belong to different socioeconomic and ethnic groups, listen to different music, demonstrate different talents, vacation in different places or never vacation at all—and these are just starting points for their variations.

If students don't have the personal background to recognize a metaphor's connection to the content, we must work to create the context. It's not a luxury to be considered only if time allows; providing the context can be the difference between function and dysfunction in the classroom. According to cognitive science expert David Sousa, very little goes into long-term memory unless it's attached to something already in storage (2005). If we want students to move new ideas and skills into long-term memory—not merely repeat it for a test then forget it—then one of our best strategies is creating background knowledge. In the case of the poem that begins this chapter, adequate preparation for understanding the references to the Renaissance period is necessary for two key tenets of long-term learning: making sense of the material and developing a meaningful context (Sousa 2005).

Building Frames of Understanding

> *To a person uninstructed in natural history, his country or seaside stroll is a walk through a gallery filled with wonderful works of art, nine-tenths of which have their faces turned to the wall.*
> —Thomas H. Huxley, 1854

Some comparisons rely on how one unknown concept or relationship is similar to one already known. There are many of us who would understand the statement "We don't want another Bay of Pigs" when talking about a bloody, political conflict, but to our students, the reference conjures a rather silly mental picture of drowning swine. Swimmers get very dejected after working hard all season only to get DQ'd in a meet—referring to being disqualified in some way—because the swimming competition judges determined that their swimming stroke wasn't legal. For those who are unfamiliar with the sports terminology, the term DQ'd might suggest a fun trip to a fast-food ice cream establishment. Ordering a Blizzard at Dairy Queen makes sense in that frame of thinking but is very puzzling to English language learners. The degree of the listener's successful processing of the information is proportionate to his or her personal history with the topic.

"He flozzled his Web site." Is this a good or a bad thing? We don't know. What if we changed the sentence to say: "He flozzled his Web site, and the fallout was considerable"? We might not know what "flozzled his Web site" means, but we could guess that it's not a positive action because we understand that "fallout" usually refers to bad things, such as the radioactive aftermath of a nuclear detonation. We create context for understanding the unknown verb *flozzled* through reference to the fallout metaphor. Students must have enough personal background to engage in such metaphorical connections. One of the great insights of teaching is how much learning occurs when we provide students with experiences that help them build a framework for analytical thinking.

Patty Kinney, associate director for middle level services at the National Association of Secondary School Principals, provided further insight on how students' backgrounds impact their capacity to learn. Some families, she said, relate to each other in ways that do not provide the thinking experiences needed for school success. For example, some parents do not explain their rationale for rules of conduct. When a child asks for a snack before dinner, parents might say "No" without elaboration. In other families, however, children get an explanation such as, "No, you cannot have a snack so close to dinner. It will ruin your appetite." Children in these families learn that there are consequences for actions and learn about the nature of cause and effect. The first family's children do not receive reinforcement of this simple sequence. As a result, they may founder in academic situations in which they are asked to analyze the cause/effect relationship between two people or events or to create a cause-and-effect graphic organizer—a virtual metaphor of information. They are not able to play this part in the game of school because they don't have the frame of reference.

If we want the information to make sense and move into students' long-term memory, we need to show them how metaphors and analogies can transfer concrete knowledge to abstract ideas or provide a map between seemingly disconnected concepts. For example, a simple, declarative sentence such as "The blonde was beautiful" is a minimally descriptive statement that probably won't linger beyond short-term memory. But it's hard to forget that same idea when detective fiction writer Raymond Chandler includes this vivid metaphor: "It was a blonde. A blonde to make a bishop kick a hole in a stained glass window" (1992, 93).

Or consider students' frame of reference for personification, a form of metaphor. Young children are comfortable assigning human traits to animals because they are alive like us: *Sly as a fox. Wise as an owl.* And Wilbur the pig has a deep friendship with a spider in *Charlotte's Web.* But if the teacher presented a lesson about architecture and described a building as *imposing* or *austere* or *welcoming*, the students might find the image jarring because they are not accustomed to thinking of buildings and other inanimate objects as having feelings. In truth, it is our emotional reaction to a building, our feeling when we are approaching it or inside it, that creates the metaphor. That connection must be clarified for students.

Jerome Feldman explains that we don't get unnerved by new members of known categories because we have a sense of the larger category of things, the big picture into which everything fits. We can predict and understand that this new creature or concept is reasonable because it shares characteristics with others in the category and, therefore, is legitimate: "Hearing all sorts of different-looking [canines] referred to as dogs definitely helps the child structure his or her world" (Feldman 2008, 187).

This is not to say we want to avoid thinking creatively with students and that jarring descriptions don't have a role in successful classrooms. The point is that we should use the comparisons only if students have the background to make sense of them.

Creating Background Knowledge When There Is None

Constructing background knowledge, or context, is so important to learning that successful teachers make it a regular part of curricular planning. For example, before expecting students to grasp the many influential contributions that the Phoenicians made to civilizations around the world, we must explain the connections to evolving and contemporary cultures. The Code of Hammurabi was one of the first artifacts we've found to list formal laws for citizens, as well as the consequences for breaking them. Because the code was publicly displayed, Babylonian rulers couldn't inconsistently apply the laws to suit their personal interests. Abuses still occurred, but the precedent for transparent government was established. The code laid the foundation for England's Magna Carta centuries later, which in turn shaped the principles of constitutional law that democratic nations practice today. Knowledge of this legal and political genesis helps students appreciate the complexity and stability of our country's laws and helps them create and understand analogies that reference them.

Teachers don't want to include material beyond the curriculum just to teach a portion of the curriculum—there's already too much packed into one year. On the other hand, if students are going to move information into long-term memory, they need the personal background on which to hook the new learning. We must strike a balance.

There are times when we can quickly or spontaneously create the background knowledge needed for a later metaphorical connection. Consider this scenario: Before reading a book about a military campaign or a murder mystery with references to chess, the teacher and a selected student spend a few minutes playing the game in front of the class, narrating as they select their moves and react to their opponent. This way, students get to experience the suspense and the strategic maneuvers necessary to win; the historical or literary metaphors involving chess, which they encounter as they study the military campaign or read the mystery, will thus make sense. Most of the time, however, we will want to give students clues in context rather than using expanded examples.

Providing the "back story" for a topic helps students better remember information. In math, we might remind students of previous patterns as they learn new ones, such as moving from linear progression to geometric progression, or from Base 10 to Base 2 number systems. Or, before teaching students about factorization, we might ask them to review what they know about prime numbers. Then the references and comparisons will seep into their brains. Alternatively, an English teacher might ask students, "How is this story's protagonist moving in a different direction than the last story's protagonist?" A science teacher might say: "We've seen how photosynthesis reduces carbon dioxide to sugars and oxidizes water into oxygen, so what do you think the reverse of this process, called 'respiration,' does?" No subject is off the hook—building upon prior knowledge is central to learning.

Some teachers may wonder at the difference between *creating* and *activating* background knowledge. Activating background knowledge refers to students re-engaging with material already learned as a way to get the cognitive centers of their brains working and making connections. It may mean reminding students of past experiences. When teaching the concept of air as mass we ask students to remember an earlier experience in class when they held a cup upside down while lowering it into a bowl of water. The level of the water in the bowl rose as they pushed down the overturned cup containing trapped air. This is activating background knowledge.

When teaching centrifugal force, we may ask students to swing a pail of water around in a circle vertically over their heads and note how the water does not pour out when the bucket is at the top of the circle and its open end is pointing downward. This may not be something they have done before, so we would be creating background knowledge for exploring the principle of centrifugal force. The experience creates the frame of reference needed to understand the science to come.

Creating background knowledge refers to the teacher's careful attention to building a frame of reference if it's not already there. If we're using a particularly apt metaphor in our classrooms, its power to teach students will be nullified if students can't connect the concept to what they already know. While it's preferable to draw upon references already in students' minds, sometimes the background doesn't exist and we have to spend some time constructing it.

If we're teaching students that a book's character was "a fly on the wall," we pause before continuing in order to discuss how a fly behaves when crawling on the wall of a crowded room— we imagine what it notices and feels, and how it might react. If we're going to explain to students that a political party made the "opening salvo" in a contentious debate, we'll take the time to show a film clip, read an excerpt, or symbolically portray the military's first strike. Of course, it's not just knowledge of cultural idioms that we have to clarify with students; it's most of the instructional metaphors we use. If a metaphor is worth using, so is building the background necessary for students to feel the force of its impact. Anyone who doubts the veracity of this statement need only to wonder at what learning actually happens when the teacher incorporates metaphors and analogies without regard to students' backgrounds:

Ms. Green: So these elements were stacked in concentric sets like Babushka dolls.

Student #1: Like what?

Ms. Green: You know, those wooden dolls from Russia many of us played with when we were younger. They looked like Weebles.

Student #2: Weebles? What's a Weeble? I never had a Weeble or a wooden doll, Ms. Green.

Student #3: How do you say it, "Bab-ush-ka?" That sounds alien.

Ms. Green: Well, how about that magic trick with cups and red, foam balls—you know, when you stack them?

Student #1: I always wondered how they get the balls through the bottoms of the cups.

Student #4: I haven't seen that trick. Can you do it now?

Student #1: What's "concentric" mean?

Ms. Green: You know, like circles on an archery target. Okay, let's take a look at tonight's homework . . .

In this scenario, the comparisons not only didn't work, they seemed to further confuse the students. Strategic employment of meaningful metaphors is what we're after, not just using metaphors for the sake of using metaphors.

Building background knowledge is particularly important when teaching in diverse classrooms. Some students may have never played Whac-A-Mole, so we need to take time to explain it when discussing current events involving military commanders referring to reallocating resources and dealing with insurgencies overseas as playing a losing game of Whac-A-Mole. Some students have never noticed the oil and vinegar in Italian salad dressing separating from one another according to density, so we bring in Italian dressing, shake it up, then let it sit still for while, just so they can fully appreciate the analogies we've drawn about oil and vinegar never mixing. If we find out that a subset of students has never experienced central air conditioning in their homes or what a thermostat does, we pull them to one side and discuss it with them before asking them to incorporate the analogy in their writing assignment on how reptiles and mammals differ in how they maintain proper body temperature in varying environments.

Connecting the Dots in Students' Backgrounds

Because metaphors and analogies are really about meaning making, and meaning making is the primary goal for classroom instruction, we can easily see the importance of: (1) being aware of students' backgrounds as we choose and use metaphors and analogies, and (2) creating the background knowledge that will enable students to use the intended metaphor for deeper meaning.

While listening to the Kojo Nnamdi radio show on National Public Radio last year, I heard one of his guests, the director of a Washington, D.C., art gallery, say that art is really a conversation. Nnamdi and the other guests agreed with the curator, but no one elaborated on the idea; they moved to a new topic. I was left pondering the connection: How is art a conversation? Who are the two or more players needed for a conversation—viewer and artist? What do they talk about? Is art like an abstract conversation between two machines or two different disciplines such as sports and politics? What are the unique characteristics of a conversation that we replicate when viewing art? What is it about art that makes it so interactive as to become a conversation? Do I understand art enough to understand this comparison? Have I ever "talked" with a piece of fine art? Is the reverse also true—can conversations be forms of art? As one who has little experience in professionally viewing artwork, I don't feel I understood the significance of the director's observation and, as a result, I missed something others understood readily. I wish Nnamdi had taken the time to explore the metaphor—I might view art in new and meaningful ways.

Though they may not verbalize it so directly, students are pleading for clarity as well. Perhaps they've heard us refer to a historical figure's plan for prosperity as a blueprint for change. Or maybe a metaphor suggested that DNA is a blueprint for growing a human body. Or a bulleted outline is the blueprint for a well-crafted essay or math protocol. "Blueprint" sets the tone and purpose for each of these topics, but without awareness of the word's origin from the architectural design world, it's instructional clutter. If we use it, we better filter the murky water for students who came without a sieve.

To keep our instruction clean for students, we have to connect the dots, or at least offer tools that students can use to build their own connections. This means being aware of the metaphors we use and pointing them out to students along the way. It also means consciously incorporating metaphors into our lessons and evaluating their impact on students' learning as we teach. We don't formally assess each time, but we keep an eye on the overall effect. Other chapters will explore this process in more detail. Here I want to emphasize the importance of identifying students' personal backgrounds as part of setting the context for metaphors, as well as how to fill in gaps that might exist.

Knowing What They Know

Preassessing students' skills and knowledge is standard operating procedure for most successful teachers. We identify the lesson's objectives, design a summative assessment that will provide ample evidence that students have learned those objectives, and then we design the instructional sequence, periodically weaving in formative assessments that will help us determine students' progress. From those preassessments, we may have discovered areas of strength, and that foundation supports tiers of effective metaphors that we offer later in the lesson.

But what can we do in the midst of a lesson when we want to use an analogy or metaphor, yet we're not sure if students will understand the connection? How do we identify personal links to learning?

Consider using the student survey in Figure 4.1. Remember that this is a little different from other student surveys, because we are looking for specific information that will assist us in identifying good metaphor fodder.

With information such as this, we can make a lot of connections between the curriculum and students' lives. For instance, in the last question on the survey about what students notice as they enter public spaces, if a student comments that she first notices who is clustered in small groups and why they might be gathered like that, we might surmise that she is a social observer, aware of cliques, status, identifying oneself with a group, and the need to belong. We could draw analogies between the clustering behavior of social groups when teaching that student about chemical bonding, reactions to the United States' involvement in other countries' sectarian conflicts, smaller plants thriving under the protective canopy of tall trees, how some poets rarely venture beyond comfortable topics, and how fractal patterns evolve around specified target points on the computer screen. We've not only facilitated a connection between the student and the information, we've opened our own minds to original perspectives. Generating metaphors based on student background gives dimension to our own interpretations as well.

Some secondary teachers may wonder how they could possibly keep track of all this information about each of their students. In truth, we can't. Most of us can't make a mental scan of the data every time we need it. However, we can read through the responses a few times a year, reminding ourselves of individual characteristics and maybe triggering new connections. In addition, if we're struggling to reach a particular student, we can go to his or her survey data and consider how we might forge new alliances.

Of course, another way to get to know students well is to spend significant time with them. As you feel comfortable and have time, take opportunities to eat lunch with students; sponsor school clubs; coach sports; lead advisory experiences; serve as a mentor; guide service projects; perform in the school play; invite students to assist you in the classroom (including coteaching); attend some of the special events in their lives (celebrations, sporting events, performances, naturalization ceremonies, bar/bat mitzvah); put together the school newspaper, literary magazine, or yearbook with them; go on field trips with them; and take groups of students hiking on the weekends. When we interact with students outside the classroom, we can

Figure 4.1 Student Background Survey for Use When Generating Meaningful Metaphors

[*Note that there is not enough space after each prompt in this example for students to record their responses fully. This example is provided to give you suggestions that you can incorporate into your own version.*]

Name: _____

Circle One: Male   Female   Age: _____

Address: _____

_____

What language does your family speak predominantly while at home? _____

A. Travel
1. Have you ever traveled outside of our town/city/community, but within the state or province?
2. If so, list where you've traveled within the state/province:
3. Where have you traveled outside of the state/province? (If you haven't traveled that far, skip this question.)
4. Where have you traveled outside of the country? (If you haven't traveled that far, skip this question.)

B. Family
1. Describe your family, including extended family members who live with you as well as older siblings who may have left your home—names, ages, roles:
2. Describe your parents' jobs:
3. Describe two memories of your family or a specific family member from earlier in your childhood:

C. Interests
1. List your favorite sports (no more than five):
2. How do you like to spend your free time after school?
3. How do you like to spend your free time during holidays or school vacations?
4. What kind of music do you like?
5. If we decided to remove most of the subjects taught in school and limit your learning to just two or three subjects you would be taught every day for large chunks of time, which two or three subjects would you most enjoy?
6. Do you collect anything? If so, what?
7. What do you think you are good at doing?
8. List your favorite television shows, movies, and Web sites—no more than five in each category:

T.V. Shows	Movies	Web sites

9. List two individuals, alive or dead, whom you admire in some way, and briefly explain why you do (one to three sentences only):
10. List up to ten books you've read in your life in which you remember most of what happened or what they were about.
11. List up to ten current events happening nationally or internationally in which you have moderate or great interest.
12. Identify in which form (or forms) you most like to communicate with others: blog, text messaging, written letter through the postal service, e-mail, Facebook postings, phone call, dance, artwork (drawing, sculpture, painting, other), creative writing, expository writing, singing, performing music, performing drama.
13. Would you rather spend your time pulling things apart so you can see how they work, or would you rather spend your time trying to put things together to see if you can create something new? Explain your choice.
14. Finally, choose any public place in which people gather, such as a school, a festival, a church/synagogue/mosque, a shopping mall, a sports game, an airport, a public swimming pool, the beach, a birthday party, etc. Once you've chosen it, list three things you tend to notice or think about first when entering this place. For example, when entering a crowded doctor's office, we might notice who looks really sick so we don't sit next to them, if there are any empty seats near the magazines so we can easily reach them, and how long the waiting list is on the sign-in clipboard so we know whether or not it will be a long wait.
Which public place did you choose?
What three things do you tend to notice first when entering this place?

add to our reservoir of knowledge. From that pool, more metaphorical possibilities will emerge.

I used to keep a manila folder of information about each student, and I routinely had 170 students to track at any given time. The folders were a receptacle of important data—insights about learning styles, interests, personal triumphs, different nationalities, hobbies, and so on. The files (and today, all this information would be on my PDA) acted as a catalyst to change my thinking with particular students when something I was doing wasn't working.

Vocabulary as Background

> *As the American anthropologist Edward Sapir . . . emphasized throughout his career, we are, essentially, what we speak . . . Sapir's pupil, Benjamin Lee Whorf . . . went so far as to claim that the thoughts people have are shaped, essentially, by the vocabulary and grammar of the language they speak.*
> —Marcel Danesi, 2004

Students who have a deep vocabulary bank will have an easier time contemplating comparisons. Students without a strong working vocabulary will struggle. One of the best things we can do to exercise students' metaphorical muscles is give them lots of practice. Teach them eight to ten new words each week in addition to the terms used in your specific units of study, and watch them move from flabby to fit in word sense.

We might teach *periosteum, hard, compact, fracture, red cells, marrow, spongy, joint, ball-in-socket, hinge, tendon, bursa,* and all the names of the bones when teaching a unit on the skeletal system, because students need to have subject literacy to engage in that learning. At the same time, however, we teach words such as *parallel, judicial, dorsal, skeptical, irreplaceable, distinguished, primordial, aperture, vitriol, telegraph, topsy-turvy, solemn, incarcerated,* and *particle.* They are not directly related to the subject of study, but they help us decipher and bring meaning to that subject.

Imagine the use of the word *rocket.* On a basic level, students probably know a rocket as something that has a pointed tip and a fuel source we can ignite, and which we can launch high into the sky or into orbit. It's usually very fast, too. This is its denotation, but what is its connotation?

"He rocketed across the field." Based on our knowledge of *rocket,* we interpret this phrase as a person running (or driving a car, cycle, or sled) quickly across the field. When we hear the statement "He rocketed to the top of the company," we think of an individual who rose rapidly through the ranks. These metaphors are only useful if the listener has a solid understanding of the vocabulary term *rocket*. As mentioned earlier, it's not enough to just know its definition. We have to know its connotations as well. Take a moment and consider the diverse connotations of *fire, table, bowl, umbrella, sandwich, mob, weeds, lighthouse, dust, puppet, river, bells,* and *blowfish*. I'd rather not *table* this discussion before we *weed* from it any doubt among readers.

In addition to modern words, give serious attention to teaching Latin and Greek word roots and prefixes. Students who know that *ceph* means *head*, and that *ped* or *pod* means *foot* very quickly recognize "cephalopod" as a "head-foot" animal and see its connection to squid, cuttlefish, and octopi, based on their anatomy. In an English class, a student reads about one character referring to another character's ideas as "pedestrian." The student doesn't know what *pedestrian* means, but he knows *ped* usually means *foot*. *It might be something associated with walking*, he reasons, then reads further and discovers that the characters are wealthy socialites. He imagines these characters would consider walking for a long distance, such as one would do to and from work, as beneath them. *So they're using it as a put-down*, the student thinks. *Something that is pedestrian is something associated with the common, everyday person who walks instead of rides*. He wonders, then, how a person's idea could be considered pedestrian—something only poor people might imagine? Something a wealthy person would never think of doing? Something simple-minded, assuming the book's character believes that poor people are incapable of advanced thought? The student's knowledge of *ped* provides the keys to unlock the metaphorical description.

Conclusion and a Cautious Word About Background Knowledge When Differentiating Instruction

Much of what has been described in this chapter propels differentiated instruction. Creating and/or priming students' background knowledge when making metaphorical connections is paramount to every successful class. But we are not differentiating instruction if we do the same thing with the whole class. Does everyone need to play a game of basketball before I ask the class to make connections between a historical event and basketball? Or can those who have played the game for years stretch the comparisons further than I could possibly imagine? If this is the case, I need to get out of their way so they can drive to the basket and score.

Differentiation is what we do when our general approach isn't meeting some students' learning needs. If we want to make a good metaphorical comparison, we may need to cultivate the soil for some students beforehand. But we shouldn't make everyone sit for the same lesson. That's disrespecting their needs and, frankly, if we work in a publicly funded school, wasting taxpayer money. So look for opportunities to build background knowledge in subsets of students, or sometimes in just one student at a time.

In order to understand metaphors and analogies, students must have the cultural frame for it (Feldman 2008). For example, if baseball is the cultural frame, there are many aspects of the game and business of baseball that we would need to understand in order to derive meaning from baseball references in school and life. Some of those aspects include: running the bases, pitching, fielding, batting (including a player's average that can be considered quite good even when it's only at 33 percent), trading players, minor versus major leagues, stadium atmosphere (seating, vendors, programs, sight lines, etc.), farm leagues, motion paths of balls (grounder, fly, foul, line drive, curve, etc.), plays (forcing an out, double play, sacrifice, stealing a base), the pitcher–catcher dynamic, scoring, errors, the officialdom of the referee, the dugout, and benching a player.

If a small group of English language learners has never experienced American-style camping, and camping plays a role in a science, health, English, or social studies course, you could show them film clips of camping, bring in camping equipment for them to touch or try on, build a campsite on school property or, even better, take them camping for a night or two. If some history students aren't going to appreciate the animosity between city-states in ancient times, let them organize into several small city-states in the classroom to experience the challenges. Whenever possible, seek opportunities to unite students by providing common ground for learning through direct experience.

Of course, we could just tell students the important information without these experiential frames of reference. But passive learning usually means shallow learning. Very little information goes into long-term memory unless it can be attached to what's already there in storage. So let's remain sensitive to the varying degrees and types of students' backgrounds, and build vivid, intellectual anchor points as often and as diversely as necessary.

Focusing the Lens on English Language Learners

I love using metaphors in my classroom. There is an episode of Star Trek:
The Next Generation *where the crew of the enterprise meets a race that
speaks only in metaphors. It's a fascinating concept. We have to watch it
twice in class—once to learn the metaphors and once to translate them.
Then we spend a few days creating our own language. Frequently, our own
language has to do with inside jokes within the classroom, but the kids
really get into it. We've also done this short unit after reading* The Odyssey
or Romeo and Juliet *and created our metaphors based on the literature. You
can take a peek at [the* Star Trek *episode] at this Web site:
http://www.startrek.com/startrek/view/series/TNG/episode/68510.html.*
—Kim McClung, Kent-Meridian High School, Kent, Washington

Think back to your first week in a foreign language class. You could hear
sounds floating out of the teacher's mouth, but most of the phrases were
probably gibberish to your untrained ear. With enough repetition of
new words and sentence structures and the ability to match the terms to pictures in the textbook, you could eventually eke out a primitive conversation:

Teacher: Avez-vous un frère?
Student: Oui, j'ai deux frères.

But beyond sharing the news that you have two brothers, your French translations undoubtedly moved slower than your deeper thoughts. You might have been fifteen years old and a whiz in chemistry or creative writing, but the language lessons lowered your functioning communication skills in French to the level of a six-year-old.

Now imagine working at this pace in every one of your classes. Your insights about the Fibonacci sequence are practically exploding in your brain, but you don't know the right words in English to share those images with your teacher and classmates. Worse, everyone seems to think you have the mind of a six-year-old.

This is the world that most of our immigrant students live in every day. And instead of using metaphorical thinking to help these students make leaps in learning and demonstrate their sophisticated ideas, many teachers reserve comparative analysis for students in advanced English classes. What a waste of talent.

Is language proficiency an indicator of thinking proficiency? The answer, of course, is no. At every stage of language acquisition, humans think in metaphors and analogies. It's our nature; we can't escape using comparisons, even at the most rudimentary levels. Mexican, Greek, French, Filipino, Chinese, Kenyan, Korean, American, Egyptian, Iraqi, Italian, and Norwegian people all think metaphorically. To exclude metaphors and analogies from their learning experiences because they have limited English language skills would be like assuming they don't know how to feed themselves because they don't eat the same foods. We can't save the metaphor lessons only for advance language proficiency students.

In *English Learners in American Classrooms*, James Crawford and Stephen Krashen make a powerful point about this:

> Bilinguals tend to outperform monolinguals on some tests of language and nonverbal intelligence, including the ability to think abstractly about language, or meta-linguistic awareness, and one kind of creativity known as divergent thinking. Other studies have shown that bilinguals are better at executive control, or the ability to solve problems that require us to ignore irrelevant information and to focus on what is important. They also have superior working memories, that is, a better ability to keep information in mind while solving a problem. (2007, 31)

Zoltan Kovecses (2002) makes the case that many cultures with completely different linguistic rules and structures often generate the same metaphors, such as happy being associated with a degree of brightness. He finds evidence of these parallel comparisons in Hungarian, Japanese, Zulu, Polish, Tahitian, Wolof, and Arabic, reminding us that we form our knowledge of the world based on basic human experiences and structures, including the limitations and perceptions of our bodies and experiences in the physical world. Because we are physically built the same, we develop similar ways of interacting with the world outside our skin through metaphors. Jerome Feldman says conceptual metaphors such as "Affection is warmth, important is big, happy is up, bad is stinky, help is support, more is up, cause is force" are understood universally; they come from everyday experiences (2008, 200–201).

The propensity to translate common experiences into metaphors to make sense of the world is something we can use as teachers of English language learners (ELLs). We not only have universal frames of reference here, we also have impetus to overrule our prejudice that students with weak English skills are weak-thinking students. Appreciating the stages through which students close the gap between thinking and their expression of that thinking creates some great teaching opportunities.

Stages of Development

> *When we can't understand a language, we don't acquire it. Incomprehensible input becomes undifferentiated noise, signifying nothing. It fails to register in the brain.*
>
> —James Crawford and Stephen Krashen, 2007

English language learners will learn to speak English much sooner than they will develop the academic language fluency that enables them to function confidently in all grade-level courses. The full language acquisition process generally takes five to seven years, depending on the educational background students had in their native countries. But wherever they fall along the language continuum, immigrant students need regular exposure to metaphorical thinking that helps them accurately express their understanding and draw comparisons to their previous experiences.

What would this look like at various stages of development? Consider Figure 5.1, which builds on the work of Hill and Flynn (2006) and Krashen and Terrell (1983).

When we ask ELL students to process information this way, we may want to start small. For example, when they compare two concepts or objects, we

Figure 5.1 Guiding Metaphorical Thinking for ELL Students	
Language Acquisition Stage	**Examples of Pushing Metaphorical Thinking**
Beginning (generally 0–6 months learning English)	• "Circle the animal in a sequence that best represents your feelings." • "Point to the place where each item belongs in the food pyramid."
Early (6 months to a year learning English)	• "What kind of weather pattern would describe this period of history?" • "Is this model a good example of how scavengers fit into the food web?"
Transitional (1–3 years learning English)	• "Explain why the structure of an atom is no longer considered similar to the structure of the solar system." • "Explain how both experimental data and an argument can be valid."
Approaching Proficiency (3–5 years learning English)	• "Why do you think the building pattern of rabbit warrens is like the design of Mayan art?" • "What would happen if we switched the object of comparison from an orange to a radish? Could the same statements be made—why or why not?"
Fluency (5–7 years learning English)	• "Retell the fairy tale or children's story so that its message is applicable to today's politics." • "Decide which geometric shape best expresses a particular scientific theory."

should use concepts that are closely related, such as government/leadership and thermometer/odometer (Hill and Flynn 2006). In addition, it's wise to structure the comparisons for students. When comparing two pieces of fruit, for instance, we could compare them in terms of different characteristics, such as skin type, taste, seeds, nutritional value, where grown, and uses in other foods (Hill and Flynn 2006).

Active pursuit of academic language is paramount to the success of English language learners. Hill and Flynn recommend that teachers identify the function of language in specific lessons and then focus extra attention on students who need to learn those words. When comparing or contrasting two topics, additional time should be spent teaching students the meaning of "instead of," "on the other hand," "not only," "while," "yet," "although," "similarly," "unlike," and, "however." If we're classifying something in math or science classes, we give extra attention to: "similar to," "shares," "same," "common," "distinct," "feature," "trait," "characteristic," "type," "greater than," and "equal." If language is being used to persuade, we focus on "evidence," "claim," "in my opinion," "as a result," "in order to," "argue," "benefit," "weak," "due to," and "because." It would be easy to assume all students knew these terms and concepts, but these actions—compare/contrast, classification, and persuasion—require implicit knowledge of their specific lexicons, and few of our ELL students will have already learned these concepts in English. If we want students to think metaphorically and express abstract thinking in English, we'll need to make sure they are equipped with the proper tools, the terminology.

A popular practice in schools is to teach subject content to ELL students in their native language whenever possible (Crawford and Krashen 2007). This is helpful for developing proficiency in English as well as in metaphorical thinking, because we only remember concepts that we can understand. Teaching students thoughtfully in their native language helps them develop deeper understanding of the topic.

As students become proficient in the specific content, we can place them in "sheltered instruction" experiences in which we focus predominantly on that content, but we weave in English as much as possible without diluting full content mastery. "The goal in the minds of both students and the teacher is mastering the subject matter, not particular rules of grammar or vocabulary," Crawford and Krashen write. "In this way, students absorb academic English naturally and incidentally, while they are learning useful knowledge. If students are tested, they are tested on subject matter, not language" (2007, 24). As the authors emphasize, teaching in this way enables students to keep up with native English speakers—an important social/emotional aspect of fully integrating ELL students within our communities.

Some teachers may agree in theory, but don't know someone who can translate Urdu, Swahili, or another language spoken by a few of their students. There are several options when this occurs: First, consider going online. There are many Web sites dedicated to translations. Search for "Translate Urdu," for example, and you'll find several resources. There are also associations of language translators. Again, on a search engine, just type, "translators," and you'll see options, some of which are free. Second, consider family members of the student. Ask if some can translate material for the student. Third, contact the native country's embassy in Washington, D.C., or a local consulate and ask about translation services available for families from their country. Embassies can be busy places, so don't get discouraged if they don't respond right away. I've contacted several on behalf of my students over the years, and I've usually had to call a second time or resubmit e-mail requests before getting a response. Along these same lines, if a bank or invest-ment firm in your area has experience in international finance, you may find people who speak multiple languages. They may be willing to assist you with small projects or help you find a local translator.

Don't forget about local associations of people from the specific culture in question. They often have liaisons with the larger community and can con-tact their membership to find someone who can help with translations. Finally, remember that the future is now: new technology devices, often pocket-sized, can translate almost any language into English and back again. See if your school can invest in a few tools for students.

Multiple Word Meanings for ELLs

Many words in the English language have multiple and diverse meanings, which makes the dictionary a useful metaphor resource. Exploring some examples can strengthen students' metaphorical thinking. These activities are great for all students, but they can be particularly helpful for English lan-guage learners who are building academic vocabulary and trying to grasp the nuances of their new tongue.

Consider the various connotations of these terms: *cook, light, fire, wall, run, bleed, read, cold, plant, shade, blanket, sound, wave, mask, book, race, curve*, and *table*. Notice that changing the tense and/or parts of speech shifts the meaning in many cases: "He *ran* a good campaign." "Let's give it a dry *run*." "Are you *running* out of steam?" "Let's *table* this conversation until later." "She sat at the *table* for dinner." "The *table* displays the empirical data for our conclusions."

Repeated experiences exploring words like this build the dexterity stu-dents need to think abstractly. Once we show them language patterns that expand their metaphorical thinking, they'll start seeing examples every-where. They'll report multiple word meanings without being asked.

In *Making Words Their Own: Building Foundations for Powerful Vocabularies*, Linda Allen and LeAnn Nickelsen (2008) offer some great vocabulary-building ideas for incorporating word play and discussion. In the activity "Extreme Vocabulary," for example, the teacher distributes word pairs that are extreme opposites, such as *thrilled–bored, never–always, average–extraordinary*, and *inconsolable–carefree*. Working with partners, students place these words at opposite ends of a continuum drawn on paper or hung as tent cards at either end of a suspended rope. In between the extremes, students place words that fall along the continuum of meaning. An easy example would focus on extremes of temperature:

<u>Freezing</u> — Cold — Tepid — Warm — Hot — <u>Boiling</u>

Following that example of extreme vocabulary should be easy for ELL students at nearly every grade level. But students will have to rattle their brains to think of what lies between this pairing: *inconsolable* and *carefree*. Where would *despondent* fit? How about *concerned, content, worried,* and *satisfied*? As they discuss the proper positioning of the words and physically move the tent cards back and forth, students improve their conversational skills, draw on visual cues, and cement the definitions in their minds.

Examining the relationships between word pairs also helps students search their brains for cognitive reference points—a crucial part of metaphor making. They start to ask themselves: Have I seen or heard this word before? What does it remind me of? Could I draw a symbol or picture to show the subtle differences among the terms?

If finding the specific words to go between the two extremes is difficult at first, provide suggestions that students study and then place in the sequence. Once they're comfortable with the activity, ask students to find the words on their own.

As they become more confident in the placement of the words and can offer a good rationale for their choices, students should display and defend their work to the whole class. Their classmates then critique their decisions. Does "inconsolable—despondent—worried—concerned—content—satisfied—carefree" work sequentially?

Because students have to defend their thinking, they learn to clarify their impressions, pushing their rationale beyond what is required when responding to yes–no questions. Explanation leads to analysis: What meaning am I emphasizing, and which definitions or descriptions am I leaving out? Why? Or, What holes in my claim will critics punch through, and how will I counter their arguments?

You can adjust the level of difficulty of these activities and questions depending on the grade level and the stages of development of ELL students, but don't underestimate their ability to grasp complex comparisons just because their English vocabulary is limited. This vocabulary strategy helps ELLs decipher shades of meaning and connection. Working flexibly with vocabulary in activities such as this builds versatility in abstract thinking and the expression thereof—exactly what ELL students need.

Follow a Single Metaphor Through Multiple Permutations

Another recommended learning experience, building conceptual metaphors, was inspired by Gail V. Ritchie, an instructional coach in Fairfax County, Virginia. Ritchie recalls giving a keynote address on action research using time as a theme. To prepare, she collected sayings, songs, and other thoughts related to time. She was surprised by the number of ways the abstract concept is represented throughout our culture, and the number of ways that, in her words, "reflect time's power to be used in metaphor":

> Now is the time.
> The time is now.
> The time is ripe.
> That was our wake up call.
> Use time wisely.
> Time is not on our side.
> We're having the time of our lives.
> Time passes.
> Time keeps on slipping . . . into the future.
> We are prisoners of time.
> We can't turn back the calendar.
> Let's look back in time.
> How could we buy some time?
> Time will continue to turn, turn, turn.
> Time is running out.
> We can't keep time in a bottle.
> Time has expired.
> Let's take a quantum leap forward.
> In the educational chess match, it's your move.
> We are teaching in a 1.0 world, experiencing the Web 2.0 world, and living in a Web 3.0 world.
> The clock is ticking.
> If I could turn back time . . .
> We are the people we've been waiting for.

Her experience provides a model for students' explorations. Ask them to take one abstract concept and find as many expressions as possible in which that concept is used as a physical object or is expressed in another domain.

For example, trust must be earned, and trust can be broken. Love is a many splendored thing, and "Love rocks!"

Compiling these lists supports fluency of thinking, as expressed in Frank Williams's *Creativity Assessment Packet* (1983). This strategy can be an especially effective bridge for ELL students who have developed conversational fluency but need assistance going deeper with English abstractions. They often repeat phrases they hear others speak without fully understanding what they are saying. Examining the connotations of words they hear in speech and see in texts creates a ready flow of ideas, similar to asking students to generate as many questions as possible to which the answer is "metabolism." The idea is to build students' capacities to see and create metaphors in all subjects.

Think-Alouds (Self-Talks)

Metaphor exercises incorporating think-alouds and self-talks show ELL students that everyone engages in mental gymnastics when trying out new terminology. As with most teaching practices, we have to take the time to make the implicit explicit. We might ask students these questions:

- ⚡ What does it mean to triangulate something?
- ⚡ If our thinking is parallel to someone else's thinking, what do we mean?
- ⚡ The character said that life was like a carnival Tilt-A-Whirl. What did she mean by that?
- ⚡ Kira just said she was going to be toast tonight with these grades. Is this good or bad for her?

After we ask students clarifying questions, we describe our thinking out loud. This gives students a chance to pause and visualize a metaphor as they watch and listen. Using an example from the previous list, one teacher's self-talk might sound like this:

Hmm, life is like a carnival Tilt-A-Whirl. How can life be like a carnival Tilt-A-Whirl? I know what a carnival is—lots of people going on rides, playing games, eating different foods, loud noises, lights, colors. I remember going to a carnival with my mother and her sister.

I guess life can be like a carnival in that it's colorful, busy, and people play games with each other. But what's a Tilt-A-Whirl? I know that tilt means to tip to one side. Whirl is to spin something around as you throw it. It must be a ride that spins while it tilts and moves you side to side. If that's correct, then how is life like that?

I guess with good things and bad things happening in your life, it can feel like you're getting tossed side to side in a world that doesn't always stay level—normal. Sometimes it's so busy, too, you feel like you're spinning from event to event.

But don't just stop with your own modeling. Follow any think-aloud you do with a think-aloud done by a student. Students listen more intently when their peers speak. Use them as a head coach relies on assistants to demonstrate special skills. This process also gives ELL students who have strong abilities in other subjects (math, for example) the chance to use that knowledge to improve their English skills. And it gives students who are shy about speaking publicly the opportunity to practice with limited risks. You might need to prepare them by writing a few notes or symbols in the margins of a text to guide their reflections. Over time, they'll need fewer props.

Twenty-One Effective Strategies for ELLs in the Regular Classroom

Helping ELL students learn their subjects and gain language proficiency are necessary steps for metaphorical proficiency. Figure 5.2 provides twenty-one techniques and tips to give regular education teachers a head start with ELL students. As you read through the list, notice that many of the examples are specific strategies for metaphor development as well.

Walking in Their Shoes

Spend a few moments walking in the shoes of an English language learner and you will discover a few things about American schools. First, many well-intentioned but uninformed teachers can offend ELL students, if they are not careful. Second, some ELL students don't receive complex instruction and assessment that appreciates their intellectual capacity yet recognizes their developmental language skills. Finally, it takes a tremendous amount of energy and patience every day to remain attentive when you're first learning a language, and some days ELL students are so emotionally drained that they can't muster the effort. All of us need to be more sensitive to their challenges as well as their potential.

Figure 5.2 Techniques and Tips for Working with ELL Students in the Regular Classroom

- Speak slowly and clearly.
- Repeat important words and information several times.
- Extend time periods for responding to prompts, as necessary.
- Avoid using idioms and colloquialisms until students have more experience with our culture. Or if you must use idioms, take the time to explain them well.
- Gesture and point to what you are referring to.
- Ask students to read text more than once.
- Label objects and concepts in the classroom frequently.
- Provide many specific models, including frequent hands-on experiences.
- Use plenty of visuals—pictures, illustrations, graphs, pictographs, and real objects—during instruction.
- Frequently demonstrate what you mean; don't just describe. Hill and Flynn also suggest that "ELLs will have a greater chance of learning and recalling terms if they use their arms to represent the radius, diameter, and circumference of circles or the right, acute, and obtuse angles of polygons" (2006, 41).
- Make ELL students feel like they belong and have a role to play in classroom learning. One way to do this is to find something in the student's background that connects to the topic you're studying.
- Use thinking aloud or self-talk to model the sequence of completing a task or the language to use when thinking about the concept.
- Use cooperative learning groups; let ELL students work with English-proficient partners.
- Sometimes let students draw responses instead of writing them; use more than one format for assessing understanding if the general approach won't allow ELL students to accurately portray what they know.
- Find different ways for ELL students to demonstrate their intellectual skills and maintain dignity. Invite them to share alternative math procedures, craft tools, and play music that express themes similar to what is being studied.
- Give students very quick feedback on their word use: An ELL says in halting English: "This correct paper?" and we say in affirmation, "Yes, that is the correct paper. Thank you."
- As you can, relate information in narrative (story) format before straight expository text.
- Spend some time before lessons on important topics to build a personal background in English language learners so that they have an equal chance to attach new learning to what's already in their minds. If we're about to teach students about magnetic fields, for example, we can let them play with magnets, lightly pouring iron shavings near their poles to watch their pattern of dispersal or gathering. Before teaching students about irony, we can orchestrate something ironic happening in the classroom and ask students to comment on it.
- Stay focused on how ELL students are progressing toward their own learning goals, not how they're doing in relation to other students. This is a crucial distinction. ELL students don't need the shame of unfair comparisons to motivate their learning. In fact, the opposite will happen: they'll lose hope. They desperately want to be proficient. Stress their growing competence, not their limitations.
- Recognize the difference between conversational language and academic language and that students need help with both; learning one does not mean you've learned the other. This means taking the extra step of explaining terms such as *similar, math exercise, vocabulary, compare, supporting detail, analyze, instead of, not only, while, unlike, common, distinct, feature, trait, characteristic*, and *equal*.
- Take the time to learn about your students' native countries. Ask for their memories, and share some of your own understanding. This engenders goodwill, and it enables you to make key connections to the curriculum.

(Source: Wormeli 2009)

If we embrace the promise of America from its earliest roots, we realize that with the noted exception of native peoples, we are a nation of immigrants. For many years, I taught in a school with students from forty-six different nations. Some years, we sent important papers home translated into seventeen different languages, and I was on a first-name basis with many of our district's language translators. Our country is definitely evolving in its diversity, and our classroom strategies will need to change to meet the needs of the students we serve.

Because teachers are so used to using students' verbal and written responses as the manifestation of knowledge, they may consider ELL students incapable of abstract or sophisticated thinking because their working vocabulary is not yet abstract or sophisticated. As a result, teachers may not ask ELL students to make comparisons, analyze data, connect ideas, synthesize concepts, or evaluate performances. These omissions cause ELL students to fall further behind, academically and socially.

ELL students are a rich source of curriculum ideas and critical thinking, if we take the time to tap them. "Time is another fundamental experience that can be conceptualized differently. We are used to thinking of time on a horizontal axis, but Mandarin Chinese also employs vertical scales" (Feldman 2008, 191). What do we lose by not inviting such comparisons from non-native speakers?

In the twenty-first century, it is no longer acceptable to consider ELL students as someone else's problem or beyond our training. Addressing their needs is as fundamental to teaching as taking attendance and making sure everyone has appropriate supplies. Our thoughtful planning and interactions will ensure that all students can contribute to the melting pot of our classroom culture of achievement. Come to think of it, there's another good metaphor to explore.

6

Metaphor in Motion: The Physics of Comprehension

Metaphor provides a way to representationally piggyback our understanding
of abstract concepts on the structure of concrete concepts.
—Sam Glucksberg, 2001

It's an extraordinary claim, but I'll make it anyway: There is nothing in the K–12 curriculum that is so symbolic or abstract that we could not create a physical comparison that would sharpen students' understanding. Themes in literature? Nuance? Neoconservatism? Integers? Impasto? Ideology? Equations? Inference? Density? Oxidation? Existentialism? Imbue? Epistemology? Ethics? Sovereignty? Taoism? Gestalt? All of these terms and concepts can become experiential in the classroom. Finding appropriate physical representations takes creativity on our part, but it's doable. And remember: Just because we may not be able to think of a good physical metaphor, we shouldn't assume that our students have the same limitations.

Most of our students operate in what Jean Piaget labels the concrete thinking stage. They have to touch, physically manipulate, and if possible, smell and taste new concepts to integrate them into long-term memory. Given a choice between reading a textbook passage about peristalsis or acting out the wavelike muscle action that occurs when humans move food from the esophagus to the stomach, students will opt for the latter experience every time. They will also remember the information longer this way. On PBS's *The Magic School Bus*, Ms. Frizzle got it right: Seat belts everyone—Let's get messy!

Moving to Mastery

Participation beats passive observation if we want to ensure that students retain what they learn. John Dewey and the progressive education movement laid the cornerstone for this proactive practice with their declaration that school shouldn't be about life, it should be life itself (Pinar 1995). To understand how mathematicians or scientists graph data, students should build their own comparative models. To understand how political theory works in practice, students should create mock governments that embody the principles of democracy, socialism, and communism. Hill and Flynn (2006) show us how easy it is to teach summarization through physical cues: "Students will benefit from the use of gestures every time you say 'keep,' 'delete,' or 'substitute.' 'Keep' can be represented non-linguistically with a quick gesture by crossing both arms over your chest. 'Delete' can be shown by having one hand grab something from the other and then throw it away. For 'substitute,' you can place both fists in front of your chest and then move the right fist up and over the left" (66).

Physical models and movements prompt learning in a number of ways. They:

- ⚡ Get oxygen and nutrients quickly to cognitive centers of the brain
- ⚡ Relieve bone growth plate stress, particularly for middle and high school students
- ⚡ Relax students and improve their attitudes and behaviors by creating mild euphoria
- ⚡ Make content vivid and thereby increase long-term memory retention
- ⚡ Are fun and intrinsically motivating
- ⚡ Provide insight into concepts previously unseen

Metaphors are grounded in our physical experiences. For example, loneliness is often associated with being cold because in many situations in which we were physically cold, we were alone, away from heat. We might have sought warmth from others but did not find it. Similarly, some students begin to associate happiness with food fairly early in their school lives. When they eat, they alleviate the pain of hunger. As a result, some students develop a dependency on food in order to feel happy and safe: They are only happy when they are eating, and when they are not eating, they are depressed. This can lead to rapid and sustained weight gain if not checked.

In most cases, music is played in our lives when we are content or celebrating. If we hear our favorite dance song, we want to move our feet and hands to the beat. As music soars to higher notes, we often see singers and dancers raise their hands above their heads. On low notes, they turn their faces downward—not just to open the airway for their vocal cords but to match the physical expression of the aural note.

When we are open and inviting to others, we tend to literally open our arms and legs and face that person. When we're feeling threatened, we pull our limbs closed, protecting the body from exposure. We make associations based on physical experiences very quickly, but this connective propensity can be a great teaching ally, too.

Brain Waves

We learn and bring meaning to our lives through the neural system in the brain. Some neurons have strong, well-developed connections with other pathways, and some connections are more tenuous. We are so attuned to the physical nature of the worlds inside and outside our skulls that we can't help but embody thoughts. The areas of our minds associated with physical movement often "light up" and provide vivid perceptions to us.

"Brain imaging studies reveal that much of the neural activity required for you to understand someone else moving his or her leg overlaps significantly with the activity involved in actually moving your own leg," Jerome Feldman writes. "More generally, we can say the following: Understanding *language about* perceiving movement and moving involves much of the same neural circuitry as do perceiving movement and moving themselves. Neural computation links our experience of hearing and speaking to the experience of perception, motion, and imagination" (2008, 5).

Thoughts influence our movements and movements influence our thoughts. Feldman (2008) writes about two important experiments that showed the dimensions of this process. In the first study, test subjects received selected lists of negative words and descriptions associated with the elderly. After they were exposed to the suggestive terms, the subjects were told they could leave, but this is when the experiment actually began. Researchers observed the subjects walking out of the room and going to the elevator to exit the building. The subjects consistently moved much more slowly—in a gait stereotypically associated with the elderly—compared to test subjects in the control group who did not study the same list of pejorative words and descriptions.

In the second experiment, researchers asked test subjects to review videographs (pictures) and either pull or push away the videographs with their hands to symbolically represent acceptance or avoidance/rejection of the item or concept pictured. When shown the videographs later, the subjects were asked to rank them in terms of likability. Overwhelmingly, any time they came across a picture that they had pulled toward themselves, they rated it higher than pictures that they had pushed away (Feldman 2008).

Our brains naturally and routinely crisscross thought with physical perception. Conversely, when we encounter words and images that don't match our preconceptions, such as when we see the words "solid lines" paired with a picture of dashes or hear someone refer to pumpkin pie as a summer food tradition, we struggle to make sense of the conflicts.

As teachers, we need to ensure that physical and symbolic connections to the content match the visual, auditory, and kinesthetic inputs students are primed to receive. If you're discussing cyclical economic trends, pair the description with a circular symbol. If a world leader used quiet diplomacy to achieve his or her goals, you could describe the leader's skills using a noticeably soft voice, just as you could use strident tones to characterize a bully's bombast. The senses align with the information.

Thinking about this practice makes me want to ask students to write rough drafts on sand paper. Next time I show my students examples of unclear writing, I might ask them to wear sunglasses smeared with Vaseline. We'll take the glasses off when the writing makes sense.

Steps to the Dance

So how do we make the curriculum more physical for students? There are three basic steps:

1. Identify the essential components or definitions of whatever you're teaching.
2. Develop physical representations as metaphors and share them with the class.
3. Ask students to critique the metaphorical physical representations for accuracy, comprehensiveness, appropriateness, and clarity. Let them suggest improvements whenever possible.

Notice that all three of the steps help students learn. They could all be used independently of one another. Used together in this sequence, however, they become particularly effective.

In the first step, students isolate critical attributes. As anyone who has studied Bloom's Taxonomy knows, such analysis represents one of the highest forms of learning. Recall the discussion of Eurocentrism in Chapter 3. What do we find when we break the term *Eurocentric* into parts? *Euro* means "having to do with Europe"; *centric* means "central." When we first attempt this deconstruction, we could model the steps for students, and then ask them to use the same approach with subsequent topics. For example, *Eurocentric* refers to the world view of people from the continent of Europe, which was once the historically dominant culture. The Eurocentric view often considered other perspectives and cultures to be inferior and provided justification for imperialistic or interventionist policies. Eurocentrism also influenced literature and the arts for centuries.

In the second step, students negotiate with classmates or reflect individually about how to portray each of the smaller components they have identified. Again, the teacher will want to model this first: returning to the example of *Eurocentric*, dressing in costume that expresses multiple European cultures (*Euro*) and stepping in and out of a circle in the center of the room (*centric*) might work. How could we create physical metaphors to represent this term? Perhaps we could hold binoculars with "Europe only" written on the side. Or perhaps we could juxtapose a picture of a wise and practical Shaman from a tribal group in an African veldt with a transparency that included labels such as "primitive," "ignorant," and other denigrating terms and symbols used by European scholars and government officials during a period. To reinforce the idea that the European perspective was the preferred view, we could place small placards with five cultural developments (one European and four from civilizations such as a Chinese dynasty or the ancient Mayans) and then sweep all but the European idea into the trash bin. Or we could represent Europe as the sun and show other countries and cultures orbiting its central heat, as planets do in our solar system. Thus, we would physically and emotionally elevate the European idea to a place of prominence.

To build confidence and versatile thinking, ask students to deconstruct and physically represent familiar concepts such as friendship, irony, and ecosystems before you engage in advanced exploration. The process of breaking down the topics into their component pieces (analysis) and the collaborative effort to create physical symbols creates the long-term memory.

Finally, as students critique their ideas and those of their peers, they view topics from many angles, employing some of Bloom's highest levels of evaluative thinking. The brain is innately social and requires interaction to fully clarify thinking and move information to long-term memory. To riff Stephen Covey (1990), it's a win–win–win situation.

To get a behind-the-scenes look at a teacher's thinking when planning physical metaphors, let's walk through another example:

1. Identify the essential components or definitions of whatever you're teaching.
    Example: The topic is *prime* versus *composite numbers*. A prime number is any number with only two factors, itself and one. A composite number is any number with more than two factors.

2. Develop physical representations as metaphors and share them with the class.
    Example: Explain to students that prime numbers can't be broken neatly into whole pieces, other than the number itself and one. If we try to break the prime number into pieces, it will crumble into jagged chunks or fractions, not "wholes." Consider that the prime number eleven has no other factors besides eleven and one. If we try to split the number into more parts, we'll get messy results. A demonstration of cutting brittle cookies or crushing hard candy with a hammer would come in handy here. Instead of pieces with uniform sizes and shapes, you will produce unequal sections: 4 and 2.75, 5 and 2.2, 8 and 1.375, to name a few.

    A composite number is a mixture of numbers that can each be pulled out "whole." You could show the class an unopened pack of Fig Newtons or other cookies or crackers that are packaged in columns. Ask students to consider what the wrapped column represents—a prime number or a composite number? Some will say that a twenty-cookie pack represents a composite number because it can be broken down into twenty wholes, and we could arrange those wholes into subsets of numbers that could also fit into the packaging whole—four 5's, five 4's, two 10's, and ten 2's.

    To push students' thinking a bit, ask them how we could use the packaged cookies to represent a prime number. If the number of cookies or crackers in the column was a prime number, we'd have only the single cookies and the whole amount—the two factors of the full number and one. In addition, if we break the seal of the package and remove some cookies so that the remaining cookies cannot come out in proportions fitting neatly into the remaining total, have we broken its wholeness, its composite-ness?

For another extension, ask students to find items in the classroom that seem "prime" or "composite," according to the patterns they have identified.

3. Ask students to critique the metaphorical physical representations for accuracy, comprehensiveness, appropriateness, and clarity. Let them suggest improvements whenever possible.

   Example: Here we guide students' critiques of the physical manifestations of prime and composite numbers, perhaps through discussion or by reflecting in their learning logs/journals. Can they improve upon these physical metaphors? Was there some aspect of prime or composite not well portrayed by the cookie package metaphor? Ask them what lasting images or motions they carry forward from the lesson.

Put Yourself Through the Paces

Try this approach now. Identify a concept that you have struggled to convey to students. Define or describe it according to its smallest parts. Finally, working independently or with your colleagues or students, brainstorm ways to portray these ideas through physical or concrete metaphors. Just as the human body adapts to exercise the more we do it, the mind develops a propensity for metaphorical workouts through practice. Soon you will easily and fluidly generate ideas for concrete experiences for abstract concepts with little effort.

If we could listen to your brain, we might hear this instructional sequence shaping up: *My students keep spelling, "a lot" as one word in their essays and stories. When I tell them that the term is actually two words, they nod in understanding, but the improper combination still shows up routinely in their writing. I have to make this separation vivid. Why not try a physical metaphor?*

Tomorrow, we'll get out of our seats and walk quickly to the left side of the classroom. Once we're there, we'll shout, "a!" Then we'll move quickly to the opposite right side of the classroom and shout, "lot!" At that point, I'll wave back and forth from one side of the room to the other and say with exaggerated excitement, "Look at all the space in between!" We'll do this exercise two more times to move oxygen to the brain and reinforce the symbolic separation between "a" and "lot." I'll even post a big letter "a" on one wall and a large "lot" on the opposite wall so students will have another visual reminder of the space between the words.

The following are some other ideas for building learning through physical experiences to get your creative juices flowing.

Dramatize

Use drama to portray and extend students' thinking. This can be done with both animate and inanimate objects or with themes from the unit of study. Students can dress as historical figures and debate modern world issues similar to the reenactments used on Steve Allen's *Meeting of Minds* PBS television show in the early 1970s (see my book *Meet Me in the Middle* [2001] for a unit designed around this idea). Students can role-play characters in a novel or political figures from history lessons. They can describe topics using hand puppets (yes, eighth through twelfth graders enjoy this!). They also can portray living organisms engaged in their environments: paramecium; plankton; and pairs of animals demonstrating commensalism, mutualism, and parasitism. Think of eucalyptus trees in drought conditions, the prickly pear cactus and blue-belly lizards living near its base, cicadas emerging from seventeen-year underground cocoons, puffins fighting for space on rock outcroppings, and a decaying animal carcass and the decomposers working on it.

Further, students can demonstrate the interactions between inanimate objects such as parts of speech, roles in a math algorithm (divisor, dividend, quotient; coefficient, variables, exponents, whole numbers), drops of water in the water cycle, notes in the treble clef of a piece of music, two important documents of a historical era, a sketch pad and a paint brush belonging to Leonardo da Vinci, and flexor and extensor muscle groups. Promote the object-as-human metaphor: "Pretend you are a virus [or comma or taxonomy, etc.]. What would you feel, see, smell, perceive?"

Students can use moving simulations to represent and remember connections, relationships, and sequences. Incorporate arm movements, head shakes, finger plays, leg movements, and anything else that will help students remember the material.

When teaching adverbs such as *precisely, triumphantly, systematically*, or *automatically*, ask students to describe the terms through a physical act: precisely ordering a range of pizza toppings from a take-out restaurant; triumphantly making the winning shot in a basketball game; systematically opening a combination lock; or automatically tying shoelaces—all done in the manner of the adverb.

Charades

The party game still works. Give students concepts to define and have them work either individually or in groups to develop pantomime and physical cues that will help their classmates guess the terms. For other ideas about using physical techniques to suggest metaphors and analogies, see *Summarization in Any Subject* (Wormeli 2005).

Visualize

Write sentences with parallel logic and structure, one on top of the other, on the board so students can see the similar verb tenses, adjective/noun placements, number of items, and so on that make the sentences comparable. Use the same method to study dependent and independent clauses as well as appositives (adding and subtracting them). Of course, diagramming sentences gets play here, if you want to show students how to do that.

Categorize

If you are trying to bring order to the chronology of key events in a historical period or explain the taxonomic ranks in your life science or biology class, ask a student to open and hold up a large umbrella that represents the larger category. Other students can take turns hanging objects or terms (using varying lengths of tape or string to suggest subcategories or subelements, if necessary) from the umbrella, creating a visual metaphor for the related items that fit within a category. You may want to use multiple umbrellas to sort items according to common characteristics.

Similar representations will work for explaining a number line. Or you could use a string or rack to hang tent cards that help students understand the proper sequence of events, cycles, steps, or patterns. Use varying lengths of string or rope to create geometric or amorphous shapes to symbolize or describe relationships such as the four main issues in a state referendum. String or rope also could represent ratios, oscillation, wavelengths, circular and parallel arguments, and much more.

"Art-ify"

Use artwork, generated either by students or by you, to portray content. For example, before coloring and labeling a map of blood flow through the heart, draw a massive diagram of the heart on the sidewalk or parking lot of the school and ask students to walk through the illustration, narrating their actions with readings from the text or holding appropriately colored construction paper to suggest changes that occur in the chambers, lungs, veins, and arteries (blue for unoxygenated blood sections and purple for oxygenated blood sections). Remind students that we don't use red construction paper because blood turns red only when it meets the oxygen in the air outside our bodies.

When teaching about "yellow journalism" of the late 1800s and early 1900s, photocopy all handouts on yellow paper and spruce up whatever is written there newspaper-style with exaggerations and eye-catching pictures that might increase circulation. Weave in sensationalism that suggests scandal of some sort ("Just how manipulating is your teacher, and are you smart enough to detect it before it's too late?" "Yellow Journalism Spreads Its Deadly Influence in Our School!"), and use a lot of self-promotion, unnamed sources, fake interviews, and scary headlines about not-so-consequential topics. (Speaking of journalism, editorial cartoons are rife with metaphors and symbolism and can convey cultural shifts through history. Consider incorporating examples into your lessons, and encourage students to design their own commentaries or cartoons about key topics and events in the curriculum.)

When teaching tall tales, ask students to record fictional narratives on adding machine tape and hang the stories vertically against the wall from the ceiling to the floor.

A particularly beautiful example of metaphorical art comes from a New York designer who was transferred to Sweden for a winter. Charlene Lam's imaginative eye, need for more sunlight, and concern with the strips of paper left near the school's paper trimmer all translated math and science concepts into an award-winning paper sculpture. For a contest entry at the Web site Information Aesthetics (http://infosthetics.com) that asked for paper-based visualization, she submitted the paper sculpture seen in Figure 6.1a and b.

Carefully look at the sequential sizes of the loops as you read Charlene Lam's description of what this sculpture depicts as posted on her Web site (www.charlenelam.com) in March 2009:

Figure 6.1a and 6.1b Charlene Lam's Winning Entry for Information Aesthetics

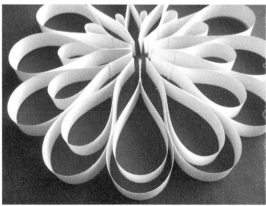

Note: See more winning entries at
http://infosthetics.com/archives/2009/02/paper-based
_visualization_competition_the_winner_and_more.html.

I currently live in Umeå, a city at latitude 63° 50' N in northern Sweden. Our winter days are short and summer days are long. Using the actual and predicted lengths of daylight for the first of each month in 2009, I created a visualization with 12 "petals." The outer loop of each petal represents the 24 hours in the day; the inner loop is the length of daylight, ranging from 4h 33m on January 1 to 20h 34m on July 1. The white thread where the loops are joined is the start/end point. Each outer loop is 24 cm from start to end point, representing 24 hours. The inner loop for January is a little over 4.5 cm, representing the 4h 33m. When assembled, like a clock, the top loop is 12 (December 1); the bottom one opposite it is 6 (June 1).

I like how the simple lines suggest the passing of time and the cycle of the months as well as the promise of spring to come. There are multiple flower forms suggested, from the symmetrical outer petals to the drooping flower formed by the inner loops, to the spikier poinsettia-like flower formed by the negative space in the middle.

When contacted about using her work in this book, Charlene was excited by the inclusion but cautioned:

I do feel compelled to point out that in terms of pure visualization of data, the petals are a bit flawed because it's easy to misinterpret the "volume" of the petals as the amount of daylight. I was primarily concerned with the medium, that is, the paper strips of varying lengths and the resulting shapes. Perhaps the "volume" is more an artistic statement about how little or how much sunlight it feels like there is in a given month, rather than a strict data visualization. An interesting lesson in visualization for me, in any case! You can see the conversation in the comments of the contest: http://infosthetics .com/archives/2009/02/paper-based_visualization_competition_ the_winner_and_more.html.

Therein lies the great instructional strength of artistic metaphor making: the discussion and interpretations that result. Amazing stuff, and within reach of our students as well.

Concrete Spellings

In this activity, students write a word in the shape of its definition. For example, *plateau* might look like this:

pLᴀTEᴀᴜ

Although words that have clear physical attributes are easier to draw in this manner, symbolic and abstract terms also can come to life through creative concrete spellings. *Binomial* can be spelled with coefficients, exponents, and math operations: 2Bi + Nomial³. Or, consider spelling words in the shapes of their meanings. This can be a lot of fun for both students and teachers.

Construct/Deconstruct

Building, using, and breaking models makes for particularly vivid learning experiences. It's the difference between looking at a diagram of an engine and actually taking one apart. An *iconoclast* in modern times, for example, is someone who breaks with conventional thinking or dogma, usually very publicly. Nelson Mandela, Maya Angelou, Norman Lear, and Wyclef Jean have all been referred to as modern iconoclasts.

To explore this term, ask students to create a model of an icon or conventional thinking, such as a specific type of art, the dominant governing philosophy of a country, or a commonly found media format (a television sitcom). Then ask students to identify the person who has dramatically redesigned or caused the dismantling of the chosen icon. Ask students to demonstrate that person breaking the icon apart: Mandela opens his jail cell door and knocks over Apartheid, Andy Warhol pulls his painting of a can of Campbell's tomato soup through a tear in the center of a more classically painted landscape of Nebraska pastures, and Norman Lear is portrayed lifting up the corner of a rug to reveal the racial bigotry underneath (the rug is actually a picture of his classic *All in the Family* character, Archie Bunker, sitting in his comfortable living room chair). Constructing and deconstructing create the vivid learning.

To give life to the diagrams of the human skeleton that students see in their textbooks, bring in a plastic model or real skeleton so they can hold and manipulate body parts. Or ask them to build each of the three major types of joints using household items.

Let students create body sculptures to symbolically portray abstract concepts. Every member of the group must be in the sculpture, and every frozen positioning of the limbs, head, and torso should advance the definition of the concept. Classmates guess what concept is being conveyed, and critique the group's tableau once it is discovered. For example, "transition" could be portrayed by six students positioned in a row, each configured to represent successively rising heights: prone, fetal position on knees, on knees with torso straight, on feet but bent over, on feet but standing on tiptoes.

Imagine building a model of the abstract idea. What physical shapes and connections would we use to build trust? Iambic pentameter? Government? Dedication? Gravity? Water cohesion? Cell respiration? Students' imaginative constructions never fail to impress.

Inspiring Analogies

The sooner we become adept at using physical metaphors to convey abstract concepts, the better we will be able to serve students' learning needs. Still not convinced? Here's a personal story from one of my former classes:

I was teaching the rhetorical triangle to my seventh graders. The Greek philosopher Aristotle claimed that a speaker's ability to persuade an audience depends on three appeals: ethos (ethical), persuasive because of the speaker's credentials or authority; pathos (emotional), persuasive because of the speaker's personal connections to the audience; and logos (logical), persuasive because of the speaker's assemblage of evidence to support claims. Aristotle taught that all three factors must be in place for effective argumentation. The rhetorical triangle is equilateral; each side or appeal is as necessary as the others for effective rhetoric. Otherwise the argument falls apart, just as a three-legged stool will topple over if one of its legs breaks. (For more about Aristotle's rhetorical triangle, see the Web site set up by the University of Georgia Writing Center: www.english.uga.edu/writingcenter/writing/triangle .html.)

When it came time for students to process what they had learned about the rhetorical triangle, I consulted the multiple intelligence matrix that I had completed earlier in the year. Through a series of inventories and observations, I had identified at least three learning proclivities for each student. In this particular class, most of the students were in the band and orchestra programs and their proclivities were musical in nature. Some were skilled cartoonists, illustrators, dancers, and Web page designers. I had a cornucopia of artistic talent in the room.

"Because so many of you are into the arts," I told them, "we're going to use your strengths to process what we've learned about Aristotle's rhetorical triangle. On Thursday of next week, groups of three to four students will each present to the class the definitions of all three corners of the triangle as well as the impact of having and not having all three aspects in your argument. You may use any fine or performing art technique, but not the written word."

Students thought for a minute before one boy asked, "Really? Anything?"

I smiled. "I know that's a little dangerous for a teacher to say, so let's set some guidelines," I replied. "Whatever format you choose, it must be accurate and include all parts requested, and it must be something that doesn't violate any of the rules in your *Students' Rights and Responsibilities* handbook. It also must be something you wouldn't mind your grandparents seeing repeatedly." These days I would add, "Or something you wouldn't mind putting on your Facebook page, or being spread virally through YouTube."

The students went for it. They worked in teams for several days; finally Thursday arrived. Group after group presented their artistic interpretations, some musical, some with physical motion, some using physical models. Then it was time for three boys to share their metaphor project.

The boys walked to the front of the classroom and faced their classmates. Each boy threw a tennis ball into the air and caught it with the same hand when it came back down. After tossing the balls silently for a few times, one of the boys stepped forward and asked the class, "What do you think of our act?"

The students in the class were confused and slightly annoyed. "What is this?" they asked. "What are you doing? This is boring."

The performing students acted apologetic, then grinned, turned around and grabbed a second tennis ball they had stored behind them. Each boy next threw two tennis balls into the air, one in each hand, and caught the balls with the same hand—up, down, up, down, up, down. After a few tosses, another one of the boys stepped forward and asked his classmates, "Now, what do you think of our act?"

The class again complained. "Stop wasting everyone's time," they clamored. "We have more groups to go after you."

Once more the boys acted as if they were embarrassed by their foolishness. They smiled, turned, and grabbed another tennis ball behind them. Now each boy had three tennis balls in his collection. They paused a moment, then held up each ball, giving it a label: "This is the ball of logos, this one is ethos, and this last one is pathos," they said, and they defined each term. Then they juggled the tennis balls.

The class snickered. They could see the pseudo-triangular pattern in the path of the balls through the juggling. "We get it, we get it," they said.

Hearing this, the boy who had not yet spoken finally did so. "Not quite," he said and smiled. The three boys took two steps back and started tossing the balls to each other, nine balls fluidly juggled from equilateral positions.

The attitude in the room didn't just turn around, it did a 180.

"Whoa!" the class called. "That's awesome! How did you learn to do that?" Students sat up straight, some on the edge of their chairs. "Show me how to do that!" a classmate called. The energy in the room rose dramatically.

When the boys saw the impact of their juggling on the class, they froze mid-throw and the last boy spoke again.

"Exactly! When you only have one or two of ethos, pathos, logos, it's lame; there's no impact on the viewer or listener. But when you have all three: ethos, pathos, and logos, it has maximum impact." Then he added a quick, "And we are done!" and the boys quickly left the front of the room and returned to their seats.

It was all I could do to not climb to the rooftop of the building and shout to the naysayers of today's teens, "Look what these students can do!" They were light-years beyond me. What would have happened if I had limited this metaphorical expression to my limited imagination? I probably would have assembled a simple toothpick-and-gumdrop triangle model. Once again I was reassured that my mantra still applies: *Let me get out of my students' way and watch them soar.*

Yes, there are physics involved in teaching students to think metaphorically. For Newton's First Law on inertia: A student at rest or in perpetual motion stays at rest or in perpetual motion unless acted upon by outside force. That student operating without connections provided by the outside forces of metaphors and analogies will remain inert with his learning and rarely grow, but a student in motion through physical metaphors will continue his forward speed. Not only is his learning unimpeded, he has fuel to burn intellectually. Regarding metaphors and Newton's Second Law, the power of that learning is equal to the effect size of the metaphor (mass) times the increasing flow of metaphor-building tools he is taught (acceleration). Newton's Third Law is stated simply as, "To every action there is an equal and opposite reaction." And for every metaphor or analogy students construct, learning bounces back just as strongly, reminding us of the old adage that we get out of learning what we put into learning: faded metaphors yield faded learning, bold metaphors create bold learning. Creating moving and stationary physical models of abstract concepts is just the sort of learning that Newton and Archimedes envisioned.

7

Seeing Is Believing: Developing Visual Metaphors

The ultimate metaphorical experience: the visual arts. Why do some Henry Moore sculptures, those massive, blocky human bodies, often have gaping holes in them? What was Moore's possible metaphor? What do Alberto Giacometti's anguished, concentration-camp-thin figures say about 20th century humanity? Why is Pablo Picasso's "The Old Guitarist" composed primarily of shades of blue? Why was Schindler's List shot in black and white? And why, in the film's unrelenting gray, do we see a little girl wearing a red coat? Since visual art is so immediate and concrete, as well as an excellent way of approaching history, its explicit and implicit comparisons would perhaps be more accessible to some students than words alone.
—John Herzfeld, Louisville Collegiate School, Louisville, Kentucky

Symbolic Sensing

When most of us in industrialized nations see the following shape on a sign posted near an intersection of two roads, we interpret it as a message to stop:

77

Traffic signs are a common form of visual imagery used to convey information. Runes, codes, and international warning signs (⊘) also symbolize meaning through imagery. In each instance, we are substituting something in one domain for something in another domain; we're creating metaphors. Words and numbers are forms of metaphors. They convey meaning beyond the strokes used to make them, and each symbol redescribes or reinterprets an intended topic or message. To this day, I have an intense emotional response to the letters *d-a-o-o-u-i-d-y-v-l-e* arranged and written to me in the sequence "I love you, Dad," in a message from my son or daughter. The letters mean nothing individually, but when I see them arranged in that order—in that visual pattern—I am flooded in one breath.

Teachers may wonder if a symbol, drawing, or pattern can be a metaphor. For example, does an illustration of a person serve as a metaphor for that person? Yes, in my opinion. Consider it this way: If we show the structure of a molecule with its components and suggest the relationships among them, we are creating a virtual metaphor of that molecule—expressing something in one domain (science) in terms of another (art). The same is true of an artist's rendering of a person. Is the realistic *Mona Lisa* a metaphor for the woman who posed for the painting, or at least the one da Vinci held in his memory? To answer this question, consider whether or not the realistic painting reinterprets or redescribes something in one domain (life) in terms of another (art). It does. In short, with metaphors we ask: Do you see what I see?

Flowers painted along the upper border of a kitchen wall could be considered a metaphor—we're representing beauty, what we love, plants, or my wife's personality through applied art. We're giving living characteristics to inanimate objects. The effect is metaphorical.

"One of the everyday functions of metaphor . . . is that of 'gap filling,'" Zoltan Kovecses reminds us. "In a fundamental sense, metaphor is a 'verbal drawing technique' that allows people to describe referents for which there are not adequate words available" (2002, 112). Our minds long for this duet between the analytical and poetic/artistic portions of the brain.

Teachers can tap into the visual nature of thought readily. Students best remember information if it is presented in a coherent structure the first time they experience it. Metaphors and analogies provide that structure. Graphic organizers are spatial and sequential metaphors that help students perceive knowledge: a simple T-chart or Venn diagram is a metaphor for comparing and contrasting concepts; a time line is a metaphor for the presentation of information in chronological order; and a matrix enables students to visualize information in their minds. Visual metaphors help us organize content, including subsets, redundancies, parallel themes, cause and effect, and a range of other revealed connections. We represent ideas and items in our mind primarily through visual means.

Some researchers (Marzano 2001) include senses other than sight in the visual imagery category. The case could be argued that those other senses—taste, touch, smell, and sound—evoke specific images in our minds, but when we hear the words "visual imagery," most of us think of what we can *see* through our optic nerves, whether it be physically in front of us or what we can imagine in our minds. In this chapter, we'll limit our examination to conventional visual metaphors—symbols, patterns, structures, and anything else that is most commonly perceived through our eyes.

Art in the Imagination

Petroglyphs and hieroglyphs are among the first recorded metaphors. From wavy lines indicating rivers or journeys to noble birds with wings folded in stiff salute to indicate royalty or vigilance, early illustrations communicated meaning through images based largely on nature. I vividly remember the rebus puzzles that filled my primary grades texts. They usually told a story that substituted symbols for selected words:

The ⚡ was very bright last night. The thunder that came with it made my ♥ pound. The ⚡ flashed through the night until the ☼ came out the next day.

Norm Blumenthal used to include such puzzles on *Concentration*, the television game show he created. I loved using the visual and linguistic clues to guess the answer. Can you guess what the one in Figure 7.1 is saying?

Figure 7.1 Sample Rebus

Answer: ROLL + IN + COW + T + THREAD + CAR + BED, or put another way, "Rolling Out the Red Carpet."

Imagine applications of this strategy at every grade level. Think of the fun students would have creating their own rebus puzzles to summarize content or review for a test. In the process, they will use the symbiosis of words and images to move new concepts into long-term memory.

Curriculum-Specific Symbols

> A line is a dot that went for a walk.
>
> —Paul Klee

Some symbols are easy to interpret because of a common frame of reference. In the United States, for example, a symbol of an open book on a signpost usually indicates a library or bookstore nearby. A highway sign showing two stick figures, a man and a woman separated by a vertical line, signals that a washroom appropriate for both genders is located at the next interstate exit.

But what do we do with symbols for which we lack appropriate context or explanation? Consider the symbol H_2O. If we have never studied chemistry, we may not know that two hydrogen atoms are attached to one larger oxygen atom to create a molecule of water. Similarly, depending on our mathematics preparation, we may not know that the symbol 6^3 refers to a base number and exponent. Skillful teachers pay attention to each student's background knowledge and fertilize it with metaphorical context if the soil hasn't been cultivated.

Take a moment today and list the symbols associated with the subject(s) you teach. Better yet, involve your students in the effort, which will show you what they know or don't know. Some content areas, such as music or science, have unusually large catalogs of symbols. But symbols are present in all subjects. Teaching English? Make sure students know punctuation and editing marks, reading notations, and other creative writing and literary signals. Drama, art, and physical education? Every field has its cues and representations. Create a symbol key as part of your visual metaphor toolbox.

Can You See It?

Let's really get into the possibilities with visual metaphors. The following activities provide ample strategies for building metaphors in multiple disciplines. Consider each one in regard to your specific curriculum.

Comparing Photographs

Compile a selection of photographs. Students can help you assemble these by cutting out a variety of pictures from old magazines and newspapers or by downloading multiple images from the Internet (those that are appropriate and within the public domain). Next, ask students to select several pairs of photos. For each pair, they can write a sentence or two that captures the comparative elements. For example, a photo of hands could be matched with one of a bird's wing, and the student-generated metaphor might read: "Her hands fluttered like a dove's wings." (Thanks to John Herzfeld for this idea.) A photo of a bridge could be compared to a photo of members of Congress meeting together to solve an issue.

Provide a few examples of your own metaphorical creations to get students started. Explain your thought processes and invite students to do the same as they present their ideas to their peers. Build the understanding that every person "sees" or interprets information and images somewhat differently. As we encourage students to develop intelligent vision—the ability to synthesize, evaluate, and communicate in multiple dimensions—we want them to learn from each other's insights. The goal is to teach students the value of considering visual elements as metaphors, as well as to provide the cognitive skills via modeling for how to make such connections.

Students can hold multiple perspectives on a topic in their minds. As teachers, we want to build on that mental capacity as much as possible. The whole number 2 is actually an improper fraction, $\frac{10}{5}$. In another scenario, two sets of data in completely different domains demonstrate equally geometric progressions. One man's poison is another man's cake. The constraints of one are opportunities for another. Dueling perspectives ignite imagination in almost anything we teach. A character bullying another character may be a thug in one sense, but alternatively, he could also be a victim of abuse. A blossoming colony of bacteria may be part of an important ecosystem, but alternatively, it could also be a deadly threat to mankind.

Let's set the tone for exploring visual metaphors. Consider for a moment those series of optical illusions in which we can see more than one image within the illustration: Is it a woman looking into a mirror, or is it a human skull? Turned one way, the image looks like a rabbit, but turned another way, it looks like a duck. Can we see the older woman in the hat with her chin against her chest (she seems to belong to a Toulouse-Lautrec painting), as well as the younger woman socialite turning away from us (Figure 7.2)? These illustrations are created through perceptual ambiguity—we receive more than one frame of reference and our mind moves from one to the other. Each image is there in its entirety, yet many of us fail to notice both visual metaphors unless oriented by someone's suggestion or by concentrating on smaller aspects of the illustration that will enable us to see the whole in a different way. What a great description of a metaphor's impact on learning!

Figure 7.2 Notice the two perceptions of one illustration.

Who Are You?

Chris Toy, a middle school specialist from Maine, recommends a technique that involves displaying dozens of pictures, including abstract representations such as symbols, advertisements, artwork, and more, across a long table. Ask students to select an image that best represents them or their perception of a topic or issue. Then ask them to take turns explaining the connections. For example, Toy uses this activity with students when discussing youth violence by asking them to respond to this prompt: "How is the picture I selected like the issue of bullying at my school?"

An alternative strategy asks students to choose an image that best represents a character from a novel or a historical figure from a period you've just reviewed. Students also could use the image to suggest a feeling in response to a topic you've been discussing in an advisory period. The practice reinforces the use of imagery to express metaphors.

When I've used this technique with students, I've been amazed by their sophisticated analysis and the intense emotions that visual imagery prompts:

> Just looking at that house, I see my grandfather. It's built like him: strong, a little rounded, and solid. It looks like it would be stubborn in any storm, too, just like Grandpa.

> The front of the car has a *Catcher-in-the-Rye* attitude. It reminds me of Holden Caulfield—bold but only so much so, jumping at the chance to get going with life, cussing and doing wrong things to test himself and the world, but still innocent, not ready for the truth. It's trying to be something it's not sure it wants to be.

Graphic Organizers

Graphic organizers are virtual metaphors that recode or reimagine knowledge in a particular format so as to clarify a topic, reveal a previously unrecognized aspect of the topic, or process the topic better for long-term memory. They're powerful tools, so we need to ensure that we're using the correct graphic organizer for our purposes. A Venn diagram, for instance, doesn't reinforce a sequence of events, but it does help us compare and contrast two or more topics. A time line doesn't help us understand taxonomic hierarchy, but it would be a great method of taking notes about a chronological sequence. Chapter 9 explores the limitations of metaphors, including graphic organizers, in more depth. Here I want to urge you to keep this caution in mind as we review different methods of graphically organizing information: When selecting a particular format, ask yourself, "Is this the best method for reframing this concept or data for students?"

This section shows some common graphic organizers. Choose an organizer appropriate to your purpose, but don't hesitate to mix and match or mutate the format to fit your instructional needs. Teach students how to make good selections as well. For example, we might create a mind map to express our understanding of the interplay among plant auxins, phototropism, and photosynthesis. But we also could insert a brief T-chart or bulleted outline next to any of the areas in the mind map to further clarify its role. Ask students to justify any modifications to the organizers as they make them. Creating a graphic organizer hybrid is a wonderful visual reinforcement for students, but the real learning comes when they have to explain and defend their inventions to classmates or the teacher.

Mind Map

This is a diagram showing the flow of one's thinking and tasks around a specific theme or idea through arrows, cartoon representations, branching lines, single words, highlighting, frames, bubbles, decision symbols, connecting lines, and other visual cues to indicate causal relationships, levels of importance, sequences, hierarchy, decisions, tasks, and subtopics. A mind map often resembles an annotated and animated road map or journey of one's thinking.

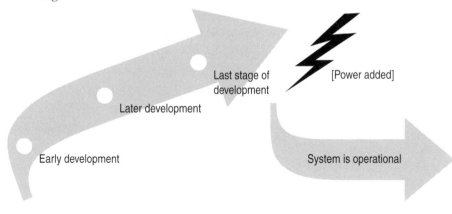

Last stage of development

[Power added]

Later development

Early development

System is operational

Cluster

Clustering is used to show subcategories within a larger one, including elements within, relationships, and connections, all focused on central ideas, people, or themes.

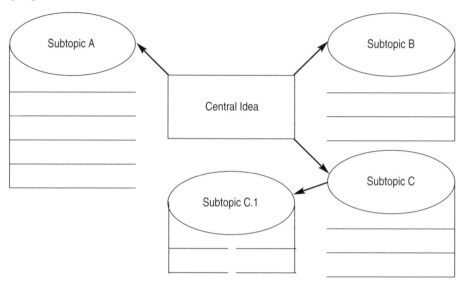

Venn Diagram

Made up of two or more interlocking circles, a Venn diagram is used to compare (how they are similar) and contrast (how they are different) two or more concepts, people, or objects, such as atmosphere and biosphere, nouns and gerunds, socialism and communism, cubism and avant-garde. The diagram can also be displayed concentrically, one circle within a larger one within a still larger one, and so on.

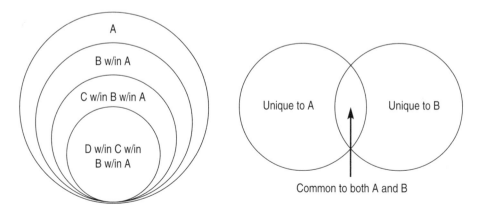

Continuum

A continuum is used to show degrees along a range of related ideas or concepts, such as the spectrum from "fully disagree" to "fully agree" as responses to a proposition, from one short wavelength to the longest wavelength, or from politically liberal to politically conservative.

Cornell Notes

Cornell notes include a T-chart with a three- to five-sentence summary of the upper portion written across its lower portion.

Reduce	Record
[Summarize in short phrases.]	[Record notes from lecture, film, experience here, or essential questions next to each block of notes.]

Review—Summarize (paragraph-style) your points or responses to the questions. Reflect and comment on what you learned.

Pie Chart

A pie chart is used to show comparative size, influence, power, or composition within a larger whole.

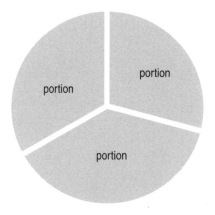

Pyramid

Narrow at the top, wider at the bottom, a pyramid is used to show each level of composition, elements building toward an ultimate outcome, multiple levels of support for something important, frequency of occurrence, or number of items at varying levels.

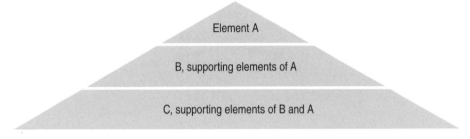

Element A

B, supporting elements of A

C, supporting elements of B and A

Matrix

Usually made of two axes, horizontal and vertical, a matrix is used to organize multiple categories of information intersecting with other categories. For example, we may record four questions across the top of our paper, but we record the answers we find from each of three resources, listed along the vertical axis. This is a matrix of information on the overall topic.

	Earth	Moon	Mercury	Mars	Venus	Saturn	Jupiter	Neptune
Gravity Relative to Earth								
Composition of Atmosphere								
Length of Year and Day								
Origin of Name								
Distance from Earth								

Flow Chart

A flow chart is used to demonstrate the flow of thinking, decisions, or steps taken. It often uses a variety of shapes and arrows to indicate progress.

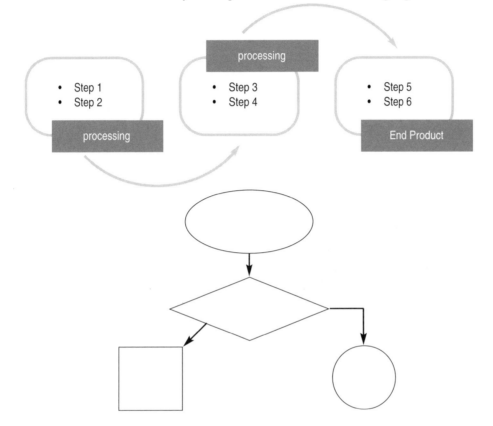

Hierarchy Chart

A hierarchy chart is meant to show status among elements, people, and priorities.

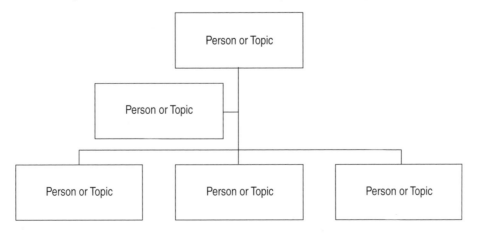

T-chart

A T-chart is used to show comparisons, contrasts, complementary elements, cause/effect, relationships, or subsets of larger categories.

Topic A	Topic B

Tree Chart

This chart is a basic tree with branches, fruit, leaves, trunk, and roots drawn in. The roots represent causes or precipitating events, the trunk represents the growth of those events, the branches suggest the different directions that growth might create, and the fruit or leaves show the eventual outcomes of the growth. We can add to this metaphor by putting knots and holes in the wood of the trunk, possibly sheltering animals, or subjecting the tree (process) to disease.

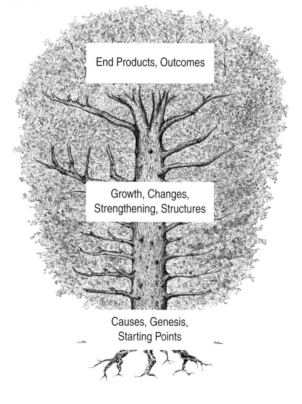

End Products, Outcomes

Growth, Changes,
Strengthening, Structures

Causes, Genesis,
Starting Points

Number Line

A number line is used to show progressions in opposing or singular directions, such as a time line, a plot of integers, or the amount of money raised over time.

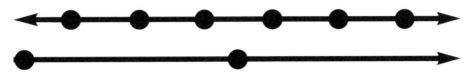

Character Trait Analysis

In a character trait analysis, record the name of the person or concept in an oval or rectangle centered in the middle of the paper. Fanning out from three or four sides of the center shape are wide rays connecting to large rectangles, almost like rays that flow from the sun. Along these rays, you can list character traits such as *honest, mature, reckless, zealous,* and *disillusioned.* In the large rectangles that end each ray, list specific evidence, including page numbers from the source text. You can also use this to analyze historical figures, fictional characters, politicians, and even inanimate objects such as identifying the "character" traits of elements on the periodic table, plants, historical eras, social movements, and types of music.

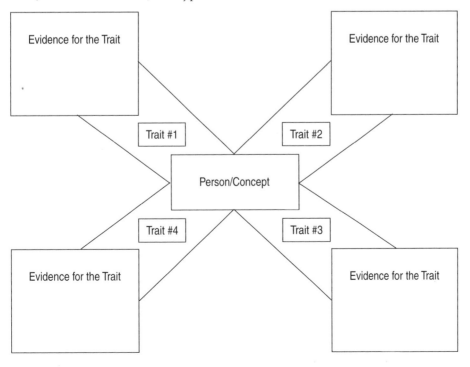

Interpreting Patterns

Daniel H. Pink, best-selling author of *A Whole New Mind* (2005), identifies pattern recognition as one of the emerging skills needed for the jobs of the future. Considering that in today's fast-paced Information Age content knowledge can change significantly every few months, we conclude that simply remembering current knowledge will not prepare employees for their work next year, let alone next decade.

Teachers must still focus on core concepts. But in addition, they must teach students how to manage, interpret, and repackage that knowledge. Metaphors and analogies are among the most effective tools students and teachers have at their disposal. For example, you might ask students to collect data showing the peaks and valleys of population growth for different countries or time periods. You could discuss how one economic trend runs parallel to another. Encourage students to design an advertising campaign aimed at different audiences. Connecting the last assignment directly to the curriculum, you could ask students to market nutritional supplements to societies that you've been exploring in class—expressing themes from Greco-Roman times, Romance literature, or the period of mass immigration in late nineteenth-century America. Imagine the depth of knowledge and the synthesis skills students would gain by accounting for each group's particular dietary and economic practices, transportation and communication systems, religious and cultural beliefs, and so on. Get really creative and encourage students to consider advertising through different themes and domains. Wouldn't it be powerful if they could recognize Greco-Roman influences in modern political satire, for example? How about the obvious allusions to Jane Austen in a wine commercial? Even better, they could draw parallels between those other domains and what they were trying to advertise in their own marketing campaigns. Learning how to recognize and reinterpret data and patterns, to reexpress them metaphorically, is an essential skill for twenty-first-century students.

To see what this might look like in a math curriculum, consider algebraic patterns. Frances Van Dyke's *A Visual Approach to Algebra* (1998) is a helpful resource. Figure 7.3 shows a few samples from the book that typify the reexpression of information into symbolic form.

The equations used by students to create these lines in these exercises are symbolic portrayals of the intended relationships. In each example, students think abstractly as they restate a concept from one domain in terms of another. This process sets them up to succeed as strategic problem solvers. As students learn to use and apply material in multiple formats, they become adept at

Figure 7.3 Algebraic Patterns from *A Visual Approach to Algebra* (Van Dyke 1998)

Choose the one that best matches the situation:
A submarine submerges, rises up to the surface, and submerges again. Its depth *d* is a function of time *t*.

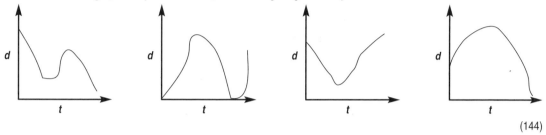

(144)

Consider the following graphs. Describe a situation that could be appropriately represented by each graph. Give the quantity measured along the horizontal axis as well as the quantity measured along the vertical axis.

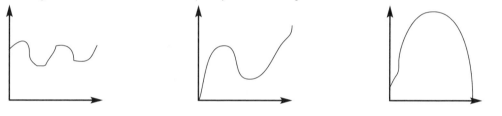

(36)

Choose the graph that best matches the situation. Write a sentence explaining why you made the particular choice you did. The exercise explores Newton's Second Law: force = mass x acceleration.

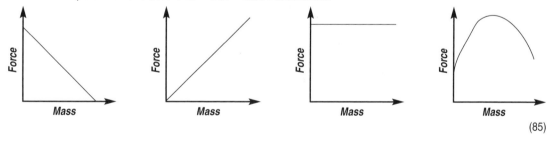

(85)

answering questions that require more than simple yes or no responses. Consider how pattern recognition skills would help in these situations:

⚡ What do you notice about the immigration patterns for New York City in the early decades of the twentieth century compared to data about the rise of labor unions in America's urban centers? What kind of lines or which geometric shape best represents what we see in the data, and if not one shape, what combination of shapes makes the best representation?

⚡ In looking at the distribution of your daily calorie intake and what we know about the role metabolism plays in converting food to energy, what shape best reexpresses the relationship? How would you change the shape to reflect a healthier lifestyle? What would you need to do differently in your life to achieve the relationship suggested by this new shape? Consider elements we've discussed in class such as calories in foods you like to eat, timing of meals, portion sizes, glycemic levels, exercise, and sleep.

⚡ In your debate about the power of Supreme Court decisions to engineer society according to a political agenda, did you and your partner come to a perpendicular point of argumentation (at right angles), or were you closer to an asymptote (a line that gradually curves as it approaches one axis, becoming more and more parallel to that axis)? What does this mean for a successful resolution?

⚡ Is the data in the table about industrial growth a linear or geometric progression, and what does that mean for the allocation of resources for the next ten years?

⚡ Describe the patterns of housing development in the area around the city. What's the best shape to represent the trends? Do the developments fan out like tree roots or like the tributaries of the Mississippi Delta that follow concentrated areas of commerce or a major natural resource? Is it a geometric pattern indicating a strategic plan, or is it random, reflecting placement according to consumer whim and decisions made independent of larger community concerns? What do these patterns of development indicate about the limiting factors for the human habitat here?

⚡ Do you agree with the message of this graphic? If so, how could we shift youth's priorities? If you disagree, create a more accurate design and explain your design.

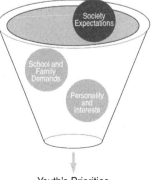

Youth's Priorities

Activities such as these build metaphorical thinking. When students practice pattern recognition, they learn how to sift multiple sources of information and recognize parallels, cause-and-effect relationships, and differences. Children enjoy looking for patterns in their daily lives, including in sports, math, science, music, artwork, architecture, and language. Just ask the producers of the PBS television show *Sesame Street*. Children all over the world join the character Bob as he sings: "One of these things is not like the others." As teachers, we can build on this interest by actively encouraging students to discover patterns within the curriculum. Metaphors give us the tools to express those connections.

Graphic Portrayals: Cartoons and Comics

Using cartoons and comics to sharpen metaphorical thinking can motivate students in any subject. Given the popularity of comics and graphic novels, we can't pass up the chance to use this resource. Take a glance at the comics in your local newspaper and you'll discover metaphors galore. Artists depict gestures, motions, and feelings with inanimate markings on the page to convey meaning about the character or situation in small spaces. "An angry man may be drawn in such a way that smoke is coming out of his ears. This is based on the anger-is-a-hot-fluid-in-a-container metaphor," Kovecses writes. "Cartoons are another rich source for the nonlinguistic realization of metaphors" (2002, 58).

Kovecses also points out the way children often personify a house and other inanimate objects by adding faces to them. This is one of the many natural ways that humans make sense of the world through metaphorical representation and play. In my own childhood, the stapler pushed across the floor was a school bus coming to pick up children; the clothespin was a dangerous mouth; a banana became a phone; a cardboard box was a secret fortress, and my pencil morphed into a magic wand. Look at items in your own surroundings. Can you see a weapon, an animal, a nightmare, or a poem represented in that spoon or cell phone on the table? Ignite your imagination the way a child does.

The authors of *Literacy Strategies for Improving Mathematics Instruction* (Hancewicz et al. 2005) suggest some appealing ways to use cartoons and comics in math class. They recommend that math teachers "make copies of key textbook pages so that students can write notes on them, add diagrams, doodle in the margins, and underline words. This allows students to engage with the text in a tactile, kinesthetic, physical way." To bridge cartoon drawing with the next steps of math understanding, encourage students to try "a more stylized representation of the same concept. Moving from a detailed picture to simplified shape, often called an icon, is another step toward mathematical abstraction" (Hancewicz et al. 2005, 70).

From this starting point, we can progress to considering math symbols and their meanings, such as: $+$, $-$, $\times$, $/$, $\cap$, ∞, $\sqrt{}$, $\approx$, $7/8$, $\neq$, $\leq$, $\sum$, $\%$, $x = \frac{-b \pm \sqrt{b^2 - 4ac}}{2a}$, and $A = \pi r^2$. In *Adventures in Graphica: Using Comics and Graphic Novels to Teach Comprehension, 2–6*, Terry Thompson suggests that "pictures are the pillars that support meaning making, and we can use this visibility to our advantage as we attempt to make comprehension strategies obvious in our instruction" (2008, 50).

Asking students to portray metaphors through cartooning helps them understand complex concepts and move information to long-term memory. Cover your classroom walls with the expressions of their artistry and analysis: the difference between gymnosperms and angiosperms, the salient points in a specific law, the sinister struggles of Iago in Shakespeare's *Othello*, the influence of Marco Polo's travels, or the impact of MASH units during the Korean War. Ideas and images are everywhere.

Use Visuals Every Time You Teach

One of the most powerful findings within the general category of instructional strategies is that graphic and symbolic representations of similarities and differences enhance students' understanding of content.
—Robert Marzano, 2001

Memorizing by association is an effective technique for building knowledge. Images that cue recognition—or, in this case, visual metaphors—give students another way to store, retrieve, and make meaning from new ideas and information. While teaching about a period of history or an important author, place a large symbol of that era or author close by. For example, you might stand next to a life-size photo of skeletal children feverishly sewing goods in a garment factory as you discuss the rise of labor unions during the industrial revolution. A book or a wizard's hat would be appropriate symbols for Hermione Granger in J.K. Rowling's Harry Potter series. A magnifying glass could represent detective fiction's Sherlock Holmes.

What's a good visual symbol of the preterite in Spanish class? What icon might remind students to focus on their target heart rates in physical education class? Can you think of a suitable symbol for an economic recession? What graphic would reinforce the proper response of bystanders who see a classmate getting bullied? And how would Democrats and Republicans symbolize each party's main themes? To borrow one more time from Kelly Gallagher (2004), why is a particular person in history or character in a novel best portrayed by a brake pedal (because he or she slows forward progress of something) or a gas pedal (because he or she speeds things up)?

Keep in mind that the visuals should reinforce metaphorical thinking. Icons and illustrations are useful as long as they help students engage in substantive processing of new information. The learning begins when we ask students: "Given what we've learned about this topic, what symbol, graphic, picture, or visual would best capture its essence?" (Or "describe its nature," "portray its character," "express its connection," "clarify its meaning.")

Demonstrating Concepts Through Multiple Visual Formats and Domains

Ask students to explain themes using multiple visual aids. For example, if you are studying the Italian Renaissance, you might ask students to symbolize curiosity, technological advancement, and cultural shifts through mind maps, collages, graphic organizers, paintings, sculptures, comic strips, political cartoons, music videos, Web sites, computer screensavers, CD covers, or subway advertisement posters.

Or consider the economic principle of supply and demand. What would it look like as a floral arrangement, in the music world, in fashion, or in dance? Now add some complexity: How would each of these expressions change if we were focusing on a bull market or a recession? Whatever symbols they choose, insist that students explain and justify their interpretations.

Many aspects of our curriculum lend themselves to these mental and visual exercises. The structure of a sentence, palindromes, phases of the moon, irony, rotation versus revolution, chromatic scale, Boolean logic, sine/cosine, meritocracy, tyranny, feudalism, ratios, verb conjugation, liquid measurement, balancing a checkbook, inferring the author's meaning, the relationship between depth and pressure, musical dynamics, six components of wellness, the policies of Winston Churchill, and the pelagic zone in marine biomes can all be expressed in terms of food, fashion, music, dance, flora, fauna, architecture, minerals, weather, vehicles, television shows, math, art, literature, and more. Remove all tethers to your imagination as you create mind-expanding assignments in the metaphor realm.

I'm Having a Vision of the Future

We can't over-emphasize the power of visualization for teaching content and metaphorical thinking. Every time we turn around, a new study is released pointing us in the visual direction:

A University of Pennsylvania psychology study, using functional magnetic resonance imaging technology to scan the brain, reveals that people who consider themselves visual learners, as opposed to verbal learners, have a tendency to convert linguistically presented information into a visual mental representation.

The more strongly an individual identified with the visual cognitive style, the more that individual activated the visual cortex when reading words.

The opposite also appears to be true from the study's results.

Those participants who considered themselves verbal learners were found under fMRI to have brain activity in a region associated with phonological cognition when faced with a picture, suggesting they have a tendency to convert pictorial information into linguistic representations.

The study was recently presented at the 16th Annual Cognitive Neuroscience Society Meeting. (ScienceDaily 2009)

We've become a primarily visual and graphic-oriented society. Sure, other forms of input and perception need to be developed and appreciated, but today's students are well served by teachers' journeys into the mind's eye.

8

The Incubation Stage: Hatching New Metaphors and Analogies

[T]here is a huge dump of worn-out metaphors which have lost all evocative power and are merely used because they save people the trouble of inventing phrases for themselves. . . . Many of these are used without knowledge of their meaning . . . a sure sign that the writer is not interested in what he is saying.

—George Orwell, 1946

Generating original analogies and metaphors is not the exclusive domain of the classroom teacher. As mentioned in previous chapters, it's equally important to develop students' ability to identify and create appropriate comparisons. Keep in mind that expertise builds from experience. One brief lesson about analogies and metaphors in early September won't cut it for the rest of the school year.

This chapter focuses on strategies to move metaphorical thinking to the forefront of teaching and learning. Get into a metaphorical mood with your students. You'll discover new connections and develop creative approaches for communicating your curriculum to students.

Instead of picking through the strategies in this chapter as if they were part of a strangely cooked stew of ideas, keep their sequence clearly in mind. We begin by recognizing how widespread metaphors are in our lives. We're surrounded by metaphorical manifestations and by objects that we can use to create new comparisons. After discussing the permeating nature of metaphors, I'll describe one of the most important constructs of the cognitive-linguistic world, conceptual metaphors. Conceptual metaphors refer to specific, underlying metaphors that are the root of whole frameworks of thinking, such as "light is goodness" and "progress means advancement." Knowing the underlying conceptual metaphors in our subjects helps us interpret people and ideas accurately. Armed with these foundations and creative extensions, we elevate one of the greatest tools for study: analogies. While there are many types of metaphor, such as personification, parable, allegory, irony, and simile, analogies are so dominant in our teaching methodology, they deserve significant exploration in this chapter. Grab your walking stick, and let's start hiking.

Metaphors in Our Midst

Building on the metaphorical field study from Chapter 2, ask students to identify and list at least three analogies or metaphors that their teachers commonly use. If they are in middle or high school, students can try to find an example from each of their classes. If you are teaching in a self-contained primary or elementary school classroom, ask your students to track comparisons used in different subjects or as they interact with administrators, the school media specialist (librarian), and other adults in the building.

Examples of the actual statements they hear and the implied metaphors they understand could include:

- ⚡ "Looking at the broad structure, which shape best describes our deductive reasoning here: a triangle or an inverted triangle?" (Logical sequence has the characteristics of geometric shapes.)
- ⚡ "Let's frame the argument." (The crux of a debate can be summarized into a short statement, just as a photographic image can be enclosed in a frame.)
- ⚡ "Stop acting so squirrely." (Adolescents are as pesky as rodents.)
- ⚡ "This character is explaining that innocence is fleeting, almost like the wisp of a cloud suddenly caught in a breeze. It dissipates completely and often without notice." (Innocence is a temporary stage of life.)

Consider devoting space on a bulletin board for a display of the collected samples, and encourage students to read and comment on the choices. To solidify their knowledge, ask students to choose three examples—their own or those submitted by their peers—and reflect on whether each metaphor or analogy represents an accurate comparison and extends learning.

Introductory Metaphor Templates

There are many techniques for connecting students to the metaphors of their lives and learning. Gallagher (2004) asks students to identify characteristics of a topic that are important enough to be included in a tourist's souvenir. For example, in San Francisco, we might include the Golden Gate Bridge, Fisherman's Wharf, cable cars, and sourdough bread as objects in a snow globe panorama. To take it to another level of complexity, we can ask students to create a new snow globe for San Francisco that people living locally, rather than tourists, would make. As students consider how this globe is different from the first globe, they might include symbols of diverse populations, elements of the city's history, commerce, favorite hangouts, politics, art, and architecture. The snow globe serves as a template for metaphorical thinking.

Gallagher (2004) and Koch (2000) are among those who recommend using sentence stems to help students frame their thinking. One cloze-type template looks like this:

_____ is (are) a _____ because _____.

To really push students to think differently, ask them to include something intangible, such as an odyssey, in the first blank. A tangible thing in the comparison—an elliptical trainer, for example—would fit in the second section. As before, require students to justify their choices: An *odyssey* is an *elliptical trainer* because it has a beginning, middle, and end, and along the way, we encounter moments of endurance, doubt, despair, and elation, moving outside our comfort zones and returning again.

The deepest thinking and best learning occur as students debate, defend, and analyze their positions through group discussions. They need to wrestle with the ideas. Encourage them to cite sections of text or prior knowledge that will support the comparisons they make. It's easy for students to say a literary character or a historical figure is like an onion, but the hardest work occurs when they have to explain and provide evidence of the person's behavior.

Developing Metaphor Dexterity

Using physical objects to characterize thoughts, feelings, roles, and comparisons shows students how to deftly move back and forth between concrete images and abstract ideas. Unpack your toy chest to find models and manipulatives that will work in multiple settings. Dr. Monte Selby, an education consultant, displays an assortment of plastic figurines and asks his workshop participants to choose an animal that best represents their feelings toward a topic, their self-image, or their impressions of building administrators. Are we/they: a shark, an ostrich, a zebra, a pterodactyl? Why or why not?

Mattel's board game, Apples to Apples, provides another excellent experience for building comparisons and connections. Using a common one-word descriptor such as *courageous*, participants must search their cards for an appropriate match. This naturally leads to divergent thinking because the cards—a sample hand might contain terms as wide ranging as *Gulliver's Travels; a stopwatch; SpongeBob Squarepants; childhood;* and *the Amazon River*—are often not obvious choices for comparison. Which one is the most courageous? Participants anonymously present their choice of cards to the "judge," who selects the best comparison and awards points to the winner.

In my own classroom, I've often asked students to generate multiple metaphors for varied objects displayed before them. They take the time to list the attributes of each item, and then they work in partners or small groups to identify potential analogies or metaphors that would cast the item in a different light. Examples include:

An apple
- we must break the surface to get to the juicy good parts
- the outside doesn't reveal what lies inside
- the apple becomes soft and mushy over time
- the apple can be tart or sweet depending on its family background
- its parts are used to create multiple products
- a star; the seed pattern in the middle resembles a star, which could suggest the birthplace of energy on our planet

A cell phone
- lifeline to the larger world
- unapologetic taskmaster
- rude child that interrupts just when he shouldn't
- rite of passage

- declaration of independence
- secret language encoder (text messaging abbreviations unknown to adults)
- delineation of generations

A pencil sharpener
- whittler of pulp
- tool for diminishing objects
- mouth of a sawdust monster
- eater of brain translators
- cranking something to precision
- writing reenergizer
- Scantron test enabler

Curtains
- wall between fantasy and reality
- denied secrets
- anticipation
- arbiter of suspense
- making a house a home
- vacuum cleaner antagonist
- cat's "jungle gym"

Railroad
- circulatory system of the country
- enforcer of Manifest Destiny
- iron monster
- unforgiving mistress to a hobo
- lifeline
- economic renewal
- relentless beast
- mechanical blight
- rumbling background for exotic romance
- movie set
- foreshadowing things to come
- a hearkening to the past

"To teach the skills of thinking without the analogy is like removing buds from a flowering tree," Bob Stanish writes in *Mindanderings* (1990, 92). Stanish suggests some additional stimulating prompts to get our brains in gear:

Which is more tense—a graph or a chart? (91)

In what ways is a circumference like a shoe? (90)

Which is more athletic—a fiord or a strait? (86)

Which has greater intelligence—an exclamation mark or a
     question mark? (82)

Which is more durable—an entrance or an exit? (80)

To get a sense of what this metaphorical interpretation experience is like
for your students, take a moment and look around your classroom, home, or
wherever you are reading this right now. Choose any three objects you find
and list as many metaphors and analogies as you can imagine: Is that coffee
cup a soothing friend or a catalyst for creativity? Is the open classroom door
an invitation for the rest of the world to join in your discussion, or is it a
momentary lapse in security? Is the computer in the corner an albatross
around your neck, or does it represent emancipation from tedium and conventional practice? Once you start thinking this way, you'll find it hard to
stop, just as your students will. Metaphors and analogies are everywhere, and
students enjoy multi-metaphor'd teachers!

Extend the Metaphors

We can ask students to reinforce their metaphors with associated attributes
and verbs. For example, if students claim that debate opponents *squared off*
while arguing about an issue, they can extend the metaphor by describing
who stood in each *corner* of the controversy. Students can describe a particular year in Congress as a *three-ring circus* with a selected policy or political
party as the *ringmaster*. They can observe a *herd* of students *stampeding* down
the hallway.

As students become more comfortable exploring metaphors in this way,
they will be eager to try out their comparisons in class. For example, if you
mention that you're going to look at something from another angle, a student might immediately comment, "Would that be right, acute, obtuse, sup-
plementary, or complementary?" You turn to the student, smile, and reply
just as quickly, "You tell me," and then invite her to choose one type of angle
and explain its relationship to the topic. In another scenario, a student
might claim that a comment came "out of left field." A peer might follow
with, "But did it hit a home run?" Another student picks up the theme and
asks: "And were we even on base?" Such exercises aren't just for verbally
precocious students. In my classes, ELL students and those with learning

disabilities have been just as aware of these extensions and connections, and they enjoy every opportunity to find them.

Todd Williamson, a seventh-grade science teacher at Broad Creek Middle School in Newport, North Carolina, invites students to stretch their metaphorical thinking frequently. Over the years, he has asked his students to compare cells to schools, a Wal-Mart store, farms, aquariums, and sporting arenas. Some years his students were too concrete in their thinking: they saw connections between parts of the cell and parts of these larger venues only in the most simplistic terms, such as matching parts that share the same number of letters in their name or, just as bad, began with the same letter of the alphabet.

Williamson says some students would grasp the more important connections with two or three of the cell's organelles, but then run out of steam for considering greater abstractions. Williamson wasn't going for an exact match for every part, just the broad connections so students could envision relationships, such as mitochondria being similar to a boiler room, which provides energy for a school's work. He found that when he required an exact match for too many of the elements within the objects being compared, the metaphors inevitably failed. To satisfy the assignment, students were forced to generate superficial connections that didn't advance their learning. Forcing connections can become an endurance test for students and, worse, could cause them to learn something incorrectly. So it's crucial to set up the process well (see Chapter 3) and give students practice identifying and testing metaphors (see Chapter 2).

Claudia Swisher, a National Board-certified teacher at Norman North High School in Norman, Oklahoma, also pushes students to think deeper by generating metaphors that describe their learning styles. At the start of the year, she asks students to take a test that identifies their learning preferences and then discusses the results. Then she places students with similar learning styles into groups and asks them to write an extended metaphor: "For us, school is a . . .," followed by supporting details.

"It's so much fun watching them work," Swisher writes in an e-mail message. "They decide after this activity that cooperative work is a lot more successful when each group has kids with different styles working together. They've come up with interesting ideas: a job, a party, an experiment, an adventure. The metaphors end up being really revealing."

Varied Views, Varied Metaphors

Place students into small study groups. Ask them to collect news articles about the same current event from multiple newspapers, television stations,

Web sites (blogs included), or other news sources. Choosing a controversial topic with widespread community or national interest makes this activity more interesting.

Within their groups, students can analyze each story from the perspective of the writer, producer, or news interpreter. Guiding questions could include the following:

- ⚡ What were the two or three most important aspects of the story according to its interpreter, and how do you know this? (To help students, ask them to note the lead and which story elements get the most commentary.)
- ⚡ Which specific words and phrases did the news interpreter use to describe the events of the story? List those words separately, and then consider the list of words as a whole. Do the terms suggest approval or disapproval? Does their use reveal the interpreter's personal thinking in any way? For example, a positive opinion of the event might include such terms as "overcame adversity," "powerful, new," "took a more productive course," "captured the hearts of constituents," "hopeful," and, "colorful." On the other hand, these words and phrases would present a more negative attitude: "dubious nature," "uncharacteristically," "downturn," "unwarranted attack," "questionable," "hopes soured," "unsatisfactorily," and "missed the point."
- ⚡ What differences did you note among the interpretations? What did some of the sources leave out that the others decided was important enough to include?

Once students have had a chance to identify the varying perspectives, ask them to list some categories useful for framing comparisons. The possibilities are endless: fruit, sports, vehicles, planets, fish, parts of speech, artwork, historical eras, movies, book genres, cartoon characters, hats, garage tools. Be sure students can identify five distinct items within each category. Students probably will be able to name many types of fish, for example, but they also must be able to group them according to common characteristics: one type has numerous dorsal fins, one remains in the same coral recess for its whole life, another has toxic spines, one uses smaller appendage fish to scavenge for food (as a shark does with a remora), and so on.

Now it's time to bring in the metaphors. With each slant of the story, ask students to identify a representative item from a category that best defines each point of view. For example, a conservative point of view may express a "play it safe" attitude or "don't expect the government to bail you out of the hole you dug for yourself" attitude. Which fish—either anatomically or behaviorally—best typifies this? Some fish are aggressive, some are timid, some beautiful to look at but deadly to touch, and some change their colors to camouflage themselves so predators won't see them. Are any of these characteristics similar to the slant of the news article?

Finally, ask each student group to present its analysis and interpretations to the class and invite classmates' critique.

Consider asking students to look through different frames as well. Here's an example of diverse perspectives on the same event from U.S. history.

The causes and consequences of the American Civil War may be framed differently depending on the interpreter. Attaching "civil" to "war" creates one frame: the conflict was a war between two cultures, two regions of the country. President Abraham Lincoln repeatedly used a different frame as he referred to the two sides of the struggle: one side was the Union, which represented the North and its inclusion of all southern states, and the other was the Confederacy, the rebel southern states who wished to break away from the Union and perhaps dissolve it. A third frame that some interpreters use is to refer to the conflict as "The War of Northern Aggression." In this last frame, Southerners considered themselves part of a sovereign entity separate from the Union; Lincoln and his northern armies were invaders.

If you were analyzing these three perspectives with your students, you could aks them to create a metaphor for each view by drawing on the categories mentioned on page 104. Which type of fruit, vehicle, or cartoon character best represents the interpretation that the South was an innocent victim of the North's invasion? Ask students to justify their selections.

Conceptual Metaphors: The Floorboards Under Each Dancer

Conceptual metaphor theory, a major branch of cognitive linguistics popularized by George Lakoff and Mark Johnson (1980) in the 1980s, describes all metaphors and their subsets, such as analogies, personification, and similes, as capable of being grouped into underlying themes or conceptual frameworks. For example, "I'm feeling walled in," and "I've hit a creative brick wall," are manifestations of the root metaphor, *walls represent limitations*. We can express this perception in many ways, but all the expressions will focus on the same idea that walls enclose us.

Conceptual metaphors greatly influence our thoughts, assumptions, and communication. Sam Glucksberg writes about many different conceptual frameworks, including crime as disease. He points out that crime "can be infectious, it can be endemic, it can be an epidemic, we might try to 'cure' it, there might even be a crime virus" (2001, 4).

Kovecses (2002) and Danesi (2004) provide hundreds of conceptual metaphors, such as *anger is fire, happy is up*, and *theories are building*. To get a sense of how these simple declarations form the foundation of much of our thinking, consider two conceptual metaphors cited by these authors, followed by examples of how the metaphors are commonly expressed in conversation:

Conceptual Metaphor: *Ideas are food.*
The metaphor manifest:
- ⚡ This essay consists of raw facts, half-baked ideas, and warmed-over theories.
- ⚡ There are too many facts here for me to digest them all.
- ⚡ I just can't swallow that claim.
- ⚡ Let me stew over that for a while.
- ⚡ That's food for thought.
- ⚡ She devoured the book.
- ⚡ Let's let that idea simmer on the back burner for a while.
  (Kovecses 2002, 5)

Conceptual Metaphor: *The mind is a computer.*
The metaphor manifest:
- ⚡ He is hard-wired for action.
- ⚡ My mental software no longer works.
- ⚡ I can't quite retrieve that memory.
- ⚡ I haven't yet processed what he said.
- ⚡ Did you store away what I told you? (Danesi 2004, 113)

(Note: This conceptual metaphor is particularly interesting because I imagine we first made the reverse metaphor—that computers are brains.)

So what do conceptual metaphors mean for our classrooms? First, we should be keenly aware of the conceptual metaphors that root our instructional practices. For example, we might empathize with students when they complain that memorizing material is dull work. Our emotional conceptual framework: *memorization is mechanical and tedious.* Sure, routines and practice can be boring. And if we overemphasize memorization in school, it can be detrimental to long-term learning. But just as machines need renewable power, our brains are recharged by processing new information. We shouldn't let our short-term concerns negate some of the long-term benefits of memorization: If I have my lines memorized, I can bring life to a character I am portraying on stage. If I memorize the baseball team's statistics, I can impress the coach with my dedication to the sport. If I memorize the multiplication tables, I can quickly calculate and move on to more challenging equations. If I memorize my talking points, I will be more confident in the civics class debate. If I know my phone number and address, I can get home. If I know my computer passwords, I won't have to delay my work while waiting for a software company to send a reminder or hint by e-mail.

As the teacher, I can take time to identify the conceptual metaphor and thoughtfully determine whether it is constructive. If not, I can change my perceptions and practices. But if I never stop to consider the implications, I will lose the chance to improve, to move to a deeper level of understanding. (Chapter 10 suggests additional reflection about the conceptual metaphors that define our profession.)

We should encourage students to join our examination of conceptual metaphors within education. Have you ever uttered the phrase, "Learning is a journey"? Do your students know what you mean and that you've used a conceptual metaphor to explain the progression of skills gained through education? Take time to explore and explain conceptual metaphors in many fields. How about an expression such as, "Inventors are forward-thinking?" Why do we think of invention as progress? Do inventors ever retard development?

Once we identify the conceptual metaphor, we can understand the motivations and dynamics within it. For example, what might have been the conceptual metaphor that assisted the Nazi Party's rise to power prior to World War II? What might have been the conceptual metaphor used by Henry Ford to develop his revolutionary ideas about assembly-line manufacturing, mass production of affordable automobiles, and paying workers high wages? What might be the competing conceptual metaphors for dark matter, antimatter, and for what happened during the birth of the universe?

Let's look at three conceptual metaphors that reflect past, present, and future prisms. In *Walden*, Henry David Thoreau decried the technology that enabled trains in the mid-nineteenth century to go twenty (!) miles an hour, shooting past the bucolic countryside "like a comet." He compared the train to an "iron horse" that can "make the hills echo with his snort like thunder, shaking the earth with his feet, and breathing fire and smoke from his nostrils." To Thoreau, the nation's need for speed to industrialize and transport goods and passengers across the vast countryside threatened his desire to live a simple, unhurried life. His conceptual metaphor—that a good life is best defined by solitude, contemplation, and connection to nature—clashed with the country's restlessness, its "stampede" toward greater gains in commerce and collective pursuits (Thoreau 1995, 113). Thoreau's perception would undoubtedly be shared by many people today who long to disconnect from the relentless pace and pressures of modern technology. But what about those who have found new community and greater global awareness precisely because online communication has exposed them to vistas they could not see from their own backyards? These are questions that students should ask and debate with a deeper appreciation of metaphorical constructs.

Moving to more current times, consider how some students cling to a single conceptual metaphor for paragraph structure, regardless of appropriateness. So they always present information by making a general claim first and then moving to supportive details. That model may be useful in some situations, but other times their writing would be more effective if they made a case for their argument by first listing details that lead to a grand conclusion at the end. Are they sometimes so blinded by deduction that they cannot grasp induction? Do they have trouble understanding that a paragraph can sometimes consist of a single sentence, which is technically correct and powerful when used sparingly for dramatic effect? For that matter, what if they believe that a sentence must always represent a complete idea? Sentences, for these students, will always contain at least two parts explicitly stated, not just inferred—a subject and a predicate—and one cannot "live" without the other. Will this conceptual metaphor limit their mastery of varied writing structures, such as the strategic use of sentence fragments in fiction? The teacher's and students' awareness of the underlying conceptual metaphor leads to better instructional decisions and improves learning.

For a third reference point, we can look toward the stars and the multiple dimensions of space. Probing the Star Trek universe for one more example of metaphors in action (see Chapter 5), consider the use of conceptual metaphors in the movie *Star Trek II: The Wrath of Khan*. One scene in particular demonstrates the importance of understanding conceptual metaphors and the danger of limiting ourselves to a single view. During the scene, the antagonist, Khan, quickly attacks Captain James Kirk's starship *Enterprise* while maneuvering through a dense nebula that plays havoc with sensor readings. Kirk's officers realize they are about to be destroyed unless they can outwit Khan. Science Officer Spock tells Kirk that all of Khan's actions represent two-dimensional thinking: the starship attacks only forward, back, left, and right. Kirk immediately calls for the *Enterprise* to drop vertically. Failing to account for the greater dimensions of space, Khan's ship loses the *Enterprise* in the thick nebula. Kirk, in catching his opponent by surprise, turns the course of the battle in his own favor: the *Enterprise* ascends again, this time moving behind Khan's starship and attacking from a more strategic position. Spock's insight into Khan's operative conceptual metaphor created the advantage.

Conceptual metaphors serve as both lens and launching pad for exploring the subjects we teach. Being aware of such frameworks, we can consider other people's perspectives and understand how their perspectives shape behaviors. Consider political theater. During the 2004 presidential election, the Democratic Party nominee, John Kerry, was described as a "flip-flopper." The Republican Party wanted to show that the Massachusetts senator's habit of changing his opinion about issues—his metaphorical somersault—suggested uncertainty in times of crisis, a negative quality for a president. Understanding the Republican Party's conceptual metaphors, "Certainty is strength" and its corollary, "Changing one's mind is weakness," provides the background needed to understand campaign rhetoric. Without the conceptual metaphor, students can't fully comprehend the criticism and either accept its premise or challenge its authenticity.

Steven Pinker (2007) and others assert that understanding conceptual metaphors moves new ideas to long-term memory. This fits nicely with the observations of cognitive science researchers such as David Sousa (2005) who claim that little goes into long-term memory unless it's attached to something already in mental storage. If we help students identify the framing concept for new information, they have a place to store new facts. Pattern recognition is a sign of expertise—solid learning—but it also leads to quicker learning of new material. Facilitating students' discovery of underlying frameworks and metaphors helps them connect new material with what's already in mind, rather than keeping the new material as individual, disconnected trivia. Pinker writes,

> Tea ceremonies, radiation treatments, and invading armies are obscure to most students, so they don't have the needed conceptual

framework at their fingertips. Subsequent studies have shown that expertise in a topic can make deep analogies come more easily. For example, when students who had taken a single physics course were shown a bunch of problems and asked which ones were similar, they lumped together the ones that had pictures of the same kinds of objects—the inclined planes in one group, the pulleys in another, and so on. But when advanced graduate students in physics did the sorting, they lumped the problems that were governed by the same principles, such as the conservation of energy, whether the problems involved boxes being pushed up planes or weights hanging down from springs. (2007, 275)

As you guide students' metaphorical thinking, consider the conceptual comparisons:

- ⚡ What is the protagonist's conceptual metaphor for life, and how is that different from the antagonist's position?
- ⚡ What are the conceptual metaphors used by both sides of the debate on global warming?
- ⚡ By what conceptual metaphor do the leaders in northern Sudan govern Darfur, and is there any hope of changing that metaphor so we can end the death and destruction resulting from this modern-day genocide?
- ⚡ How did Nelson Mandela change the operative metaphors of South Africa?
- ⚡ What is the new, post-Hurricane Katrina conceptual metaphor for New Orleans?

Once a conceptual metaphor in your topic of study is identified, ask students to explore multiple ways it is manifested. They'll rise to the task. Note the conceptual metaphors in this last statement: "Rising is being productive," and "Resting is being unproductive." How might these perspectives affect my opinion of particular people or pastimes? It turns out power napping for ten to thirty minutes is actually one of the healthiest things we can do for productivity. Resting can be very productive, yet I expressed a sense that resting wasn't helpful.

Let's give conceptual metaphors a shot right now. How about a lesson in health class? We teach students about personal hygiene and, in particular, how important it is to wash our hands so we don't pass along bacteria or germs to others. We even give them antibacterial soap to use repeatedly throughout the school day. If we ask students to identify the root metaphor, they probably will suggest something similar to "Bacteria are the enemy of health."

Continuing this theme, you could ask your students to brainstorm a few ways we express this metaphor. They may come up with samples like this:

- ⚡ "The germs are going to attack me."
- ⚡ "Eating that tainted beef betrayed my digestive system."
- ⚡ "The immune system is fighting as hard as it can."
- ⚡ With this infection, my body is a war zone."

Next, you could ask students to consider their new information about intestinal bacteria and other forms of "good" bacteria from your health class. Is the conceptual metaphor "Bacteria are the enemy of good health" always accurate? No. Should we revise it? Yes. To what? To "Some bacteria are enemies; some bacteria are allies." That's closer to the truth.

Early in my career, I worked for an elementary school principal who declared proudly to our faculty that a recent visitor to the building had thought the school was closed that day because she could not see or hear children in any direction. The principal beamed at us for creating such a quiet environment that would elicit this comment. She thought it was a compliment, but our hearts sank. We realized that "Silent children are good children," or its underlying assumption, "Noise is a bad thing," was her operative metaphor. At that point, I wondered what other schools were still hiring new teachers.

In both examples, revealing the conceptual metaphor aided learning. Effective responses are predicated upon an accurate understanding of the underlying frameworks.

Will _____ Become the New _____?

In the fashion industry, we hear comments such as "Microfiber is the new suede" and "Red is the new black," and most people understand that formerly "hot" styles and colors are being replaced by new favorites.

To tie this metaphorical expression to your curriculum, ask students to think about trends that are subject-specific. For example, what is meant by the statement: "Decimals are the new fractions"? How about, "PDAs are the new paper and pencil?" These are fairly obvious choices, of course, but we can go deeper. Ask students to create comparisons by substituting one common term for another: In government, is a constitutional republic the new representative democracy? In physics, is M-theory the new string theory? In literature study, is this character the Atticus Finch of the story? In sociology or politics, is Facebook the new town hall?

Each comparison should include an explanation. Let students critique the claims. This is a good time to model and build the skills of civil discourse along with metaphor making.

Learning Is to Analogy as Teaching Is to . . .

An analogy is a major subset of metaphorical thinking. Analogies reexpress relationships between two or more things in one domain through items in another domain: a computer is to a writer as a microscope is to a microbiologist. The relationship between a writer and a computer is compared to the relationship between a microbiologist and a microscope. Here the relationship concerns the use of a tool to complete a task. Analogies suggest similarities, such as when comparing the structure of an essay to the parts of a sandwich.

Science and math teachers use the framework of analogies ("This apple is structured like the earth.") more often than straight metaphors ("The apple is the earth."), particularly when introducing models. This practice makes sense when trying to communicate an abstract or unknown concept or process accurately and to encourage critical thinking. However, when trying to evoke a general response, reveal rhetoric, or add a new layer to previous skills, the straight metaphor can be more compelling, vivid, and instructionally appropriate.

Glucksberg (2001) reminds us that every analogy breaks down somewhere. Otherwise, the compared objects would actually be the same: "The table lamp is like a lamp on the table" isn't a useful comparison. So, in an analogy, the characteristics held in common between two items being compared can be only a portion of the total characteristics.

The analogies from yesterday's SAT exams are helpful tools for today's students. To appreciate an analogy, we follow a basic sequence: We explore the relationship between two items first. In, "light sprinkle / torrential downpour," we see that the second item is a more intense version of the first one. Now we think of another pair of items in which the second represents a more intense version of the first, but the relationship must exist in a completely different domain, and we analyze its fit. We wouldn't use "flurries/snowstorm," for example, because this exists in the same domain—weather. How about: "phrase/essay"? We might use the following thought process to evaluate this comparison:

> *This might work because phrases form sentences, sentences form paragraphs, and paragraphs form essays. A phrase is a short message and an essay is a long message, just like a sprinkle is a little rain and a downpour is a lot. Wait a minute: This could break down. A phrase is a part of an essay, so does that mean it's less intense? A pedal is a part of a bicycle, but is a pedal a less intense form of a bicycle? No, it's just an element within a bicycle. "Phrase/essay" doesn't work very well.*

How about smile/laughter?

> *Yes, this could work because laughter vents more energy than does a smile, and if we accept intensity as a by-product of energy expended, that increased intensity is achieved. In our sillier moments, we move from a light sprinkle of a smile to a torrent of laughter, and wow, it feels great.*

What about seed/tree?

> *All the elements for creating the full-grown tree are held within this tiny capsule under the soil. Considering potential for life and impact on surrounding vegetation, seed/tree captures the rising intensity of the relationship well.*

To get students thinking about analogies, ask them to consider two objects that share a relationship. Then ask students to find other examples of that relationship as a way to clarify and solidify their thinking about the original pair. For example, we might teach them about the relationship between cells and tissues in the body (cells are the building blocks of tissues), and as one way to remember this relationship they generate other examples: bricks/wall, letters/word, rooms/house, pages/book, dates/relationship, subjects/school.

Figure 8.1 includes a list of analogous relationships that can help us find similarities between otherwise dissimilar terms. I've used this list for several decades, and I try to update it every time I see another connection to the curriculum. The categories provide a lexicon for discussing analogies and analyzing comparisons. The following conversation shows one such exchange:

Figure 8.1 Commonly Analogous Relationships

- Antonyms
- Synonyms
- Part : Whole
- Whole : Part
- Tool : Its Action
- Tool User : Tool
- Tool : Object It's Used With
- Worker : Product the Worker Creates
- Category : Example
- Effect : Cause
- Cause : Effect
- Increasing Intensity
- Decreasing Intensity
- Person or Thing : Closely Related Adjective
- Person or Thing : Least Related Adjective
- Math Relationship
- Action : Thing Acted Upon
- Action : Subject Performing the Action
- Object : Specific Attribute of the Object
- Male : Female
- Symbol : Meaning
- Classification : Example
- Elements Used : Product Created
- Attribute : Person or Object
- Object : Where It's Located

Note: In addition to using analogies as teaching tools, we should be mindful that students will probably encounter them on achievement tests. Recognizing and practicing word relationships can help them improve vocabulary and analytical reasoning skills as well as metaphorical thinking. Good resources include the WordMasters Challenge (www.wordmasterschallenge.com), a national analogy competition; Writer's, Inc. (www.thewritesource.com); and a great list of categories and sample analogies at a Web site maintained by educational consultant Diana Dell (http://mrsdell.org/analogies/).

Student: The first one is bigger, or more than, the second one.

Teacher: What do you mean?

Student: You know, a snowstorm is bigger than snow flurries.

Teacher: Bigger in terms of what—area it covers? We can have a broad area of snow flurries just as much as we can have a broad area of a snowstorm.

Student: Maybe not area, but power is how one is more than the other.

Teacher: So the first one has more power than the second one?

Student: Yeah.

Teacher: Which analogous relationship is that?

Student (looks through the list): The relationship between the first two
    items is one of decreasing intensity.

Teacher: So the relationship between the items in the other pair needs to
    have that same decreasing intensity as well. Let's see if it does . . .

Remember that successfully eliminating a potential comparison in an
analogy because one relationship does not parallel the first often teaches students more than finding a perfect match. We might claim "teeth/mouth" for
the cell/tissue relationship, but are teeth the building blocks of a mouth?
Perhaps, but gums, lips, and salivary glands might be better choices. Whereas
cells are primarily the sole element making a tissue, that's not true for teeth
and the mouth. Teeth only partially make up a mouth, so the analogy doesn't
hold as strongly here; we can do better.

Consider a concept or theme that you have to teach in the next few
weeks. What parallel relationships can you explore? How about comparing
two political eras? Maybe diffusion and osmosis? Or perhaps it's not a pair of
comparable elements in the curriculum, but a single topic, such as when we
teach students about the meniscus in the fluid of a graduated cylinder or
about the infinitive in Latin class—to what in students' lives could we compare these elements?

Now consider the analogous relationships between the elements, and
what domains (such as sports, weather, or music) you might suggest students
use to find similar relationships. Walking through this process yourself
before you assign it to students does two things. First, it sensitizes you to
what students will experience. As a result, you can support them more effectively. Second, you inspire innovative thinking in your own lesson designs: *I
never considered immigration in the United States this way. Do either "melting
pot" or "mixed salad bowl" still work as descriptions for what's happening in the
States? What is the relationship I'm really seeing here in this immigration data
I'm about to give students, and what in their lives could I use as a comparison so
they'll understand and remember it?*

When students practice identifying analogies, they more quickly see them
in units of study and can draw on these analogies to better understand and
retain knowledge. While learning in mathematics that "Whatever we do to
one side, we do to the other to keep the equations balanced or equal," the student exclaims, "That's just like the checks and balances of the three branches
of federal government." Or, "That's like using the balance when comparing
amounts in chemistry class." They create their own aha! moments because
they have practiced looking for analogous connections. And when students
make the connections without our guidance, the learning is all the stronger.

"This writer is really manipulating his readers' opinions by appearing to support one thing, but really wanting the opposite thing to win," a student notes, and then compares the techniques to the way Marc Antony swayed the people's opinion of Brutus using that same method in Shakespeare's *Julius Caesar*.

In another class, a student realizes that computer files are arranged like the levels of terraced gardens he read about in his social studies book, with each tier operating both independently and dependently, providing a foundation for those above and below. Because of this connection, he's better able to navigate through his computer files because he recognizes the underlying metaphor.

There are a few important reminders to share with students as they explore analogous relationships:

Note that the order of the objects in an analogy is critical to full understanding. "A fork is to eating" is not the same as "Eating is to a fork." Make sure that students have repeated practice with this sequence and know how to correct improperly ordered analogies. They should be able to answer these questions: "Is the first a subset of the second, or is the second a subset of the first?" "Is the object first followed by its role, or is the role given first followed by the object?"

Always double-check the parts of speech. The relationship identified in the first pair dictates what must be summoned in the second. If we use two nouns, for instance, we need to use two nouns in the second one. In the fork/eating one mentioned above, it's a noun and verb, or actually, a noun and a gerund (a gerund is a verb serving as a noun). "Pen/writing" would work, but, "pen/words" and "pen/write" would not.

Students should really spend time discussing and determining whether the analogy is a good fit. Is it close or on target? Accepting a "sort of good" comparison isn't usually helpful. Students remember the ones that match.

Freedom and Power

Metaphors are freedom. As we wrestle with them in our learning, ideas crystallize; we see connections and attributes previously unrecognized, and we realize that we are not always in control as they sneak into view. This is not a cautionary tale, because transcending current boundaries is often a good thing. Freeing our minds, everything we encounter becomes metaphoric.

"That photocopier is a monster in this humidity," we declare one late afternoon in the teacher's lounge. "It's ravenous, eating every sheet of paper I feed it."

"No," says an imaginative colleague also in the room. "It's photosynthesis in the mechanical world, man, complete with ingredients combining with light and energy to create something new."

A colleague from another department steps into the lounge after over-hearing that statement from the hallway outside. "That doesn't fit photosynthesis," she says. "In photosynthesis the product has to be something new, not just a duplicate of what was. No, the photocopier is really a declaration of man's finite nature."

We all turn, our faces full of inquiry. The visitor explains: "We've invented all there is or will be. All we do now is run around, perpetuating what is already known. Each year we come into this school, to this copier, to repeat ourselves and continue the status quo. Every day this copier declares the death of imagination."

"So why do we do it?" we ask the visitor. A teacher grading papers in the corner looks up and answers:

"Because we're hypocrites declaring one thing but believing another," she says. "We keep hoping that one day something different will come out of the machine, something we've never seen before. Maybe it's an idea, a vision, maybe a unique student. Whatever it is, we hope it will escape, taking us with it."

The room is silent a moment, but then another teacher pulling his lunch from the refrigerator speaks up. "That's one way to look at it," he muses, "but consider the copier from an opportunistic point of view: That photocopier is empowering. We are able to teach more content because students don't have to write everything down from the front chalkboard. That one invention has provided access to learning for millions of students, just as Gutenberg did with the printing press. Students are not bound by learning disabilities that slow their processing, too little time in the class period to complete their assignments, dull pencil points, or finger cramps. This photocopier is emancipation from the limitations of our physical bodies."

We nod, liking the tone of this last comparison better than the previous one. "Yeah, that's what it is, emancipation," we tell ourselves, realizing that our agreement just made the visiting colleague's point about repeating what is already declared.

For the moment, we ignore the repetition because we're marveling at how a few exchanged metaphors took us in so many directions in such a short time. What if we continued on the journey with one metaphor and really shook out the details of its meaning. Would something new occur to us, and could we follow that new branch of inquiry to find other paths? Or, would we quickly stumble back to the known world, feeling safe, yet cursing the time spent in the unfamiliar tributary?

As we now leave the teachers' lounge, more than one of us is thinking, "Wow, I have got to get my students thinking divergently like this. The stuff they could create!" And just a few moments later, we follow with: "What goes unlearned because we never ventured metaphorically?"

There's power here.

9

Cleaning Out the Metaphorical Carburetor: Teaching Students What to Do When Metaphors Break Down

One student that I spoke to after [the cell-as-a-city analogy] was used in her classroom thought that the function of the nucleus was to clean the cell. This was due to her rather simple view that the city council was solely responsible for taking garbage and rubbish away.
—Allan Harrison and Richard Coll, 2008

Students can become so convinced of a metaphor's complete applicability that they fail to see its limitations and potential distortions. Because analogies and metaphors are meant to open students' thinking, not encumber it, we need to teach them not only how to identify and use metaphors, but also how to question them. We also must be vigilant about monitoring their understanding of metaphors and explaining how metaphors can break down when we put too much mileage on them.

Stenhouse general manager Dan Tobin reminded me of this recently when we were discussing the oversimplification of the pizza metaphor commonly used to explain fractions in mathematics. In elementary school, for example, cutting out paper slices of "pizza" can help students visualize one-third of a whole or perhaps six-eighths of a pie. But the pizza metaphor starts to fall apart—and can limit students' thinking—as they move to more advanced math concepts and encounter other ways that fractions are used.

Pizza pieces are not helpful when trying to make sense of five-thirds or negative fractions or when finding common denominators or dividing fractions. Additionally, if a student's understanding of fractions is stuck in the concrete stage of pizza parts, he or she will likely be confused when trying to consider algebraic abstractions such as a/b or the square root of b.

Although metaphors can jumpstart students' thinking about big ideas, we want to ensure that students don't consider each comparison a literal match. Susie, a middle school colleague from Indianapolis, affirmed the importance of critical analysis during a recent online chat about metaphors used in science. Susie said she was struggling to clarify the phases of the moon and the "reasons for the seasons" to her sixth graders when she stumbled on a metaphor used by Bill Nye the Science Guy. Nye compared the phases of the moon to a baseball diamond.

"It's a wonderful analogy: earth at the pitcher's mound, the moon goes counterclockwise around the bases like a runner does, and if the sun is behind home plate, first base is the first quarter, second base is the full moon, third base is the third quarter, etc.," Susie explained. "I added to it a bit and had a student 'run the bases' with their 'front' (the light side of the moon) always facing the earth. They do seem to understand the phases a bit better! When I had them describe it in their assessment, they were free to add diagrams."

I was intrigued by the comparison but also bothered by the potential misconceptions. The baseball metaphor implies that the earth and moon are always in the same plane, which could cause one to wonder why we don't see solar and lunar eclipses more often. Also, for the metaphor to work, we'd have to explain that the earth (represented by the pitcher's mound) is always rotating. During our subsequent e-mail discussion, Susie said that both she and Bill Nye had considered the metaphorical pitfalls, so to ensure that students understood the differences in the planes, she would further explore the spatial relationships among the earth, moon, and sun.

"I could have the kids run the bases, part of the time standing up fully and part of the time nearer the ground," Susie said, as she tried to raise and lower the angle of view of the pitcher's mound (the earth). "This would be similar to the moon traveling on a different plane relative to the earth."

Asking students to consider and solve the limitations of metaphors is where the real learning occurs. This metaphor wrangling, including the personal examination followed by a public explanation, is often the key to long-term retention of content. Certainly, it is the stuff of great debates, and debate is one of the most effective teaching strategies we offer students.

Let's explore some other important cautions when teaching and learning with metaphors.

Metaphor and Manipulation

When reading or watching fantasy, science fiction, and horror movies, we willingly suspend our disbelief to explore the boundaries of imagination. We know that magic carpets don't really fly through the air and that Harry Potter's wand doesn't really make objects disappear. We put physics principles aside because we want to be entertained by the possibilities that creative writers suggest.

The problem occurs when we are manipulated into feeling or deciding something without being aware of the subterfuge. Without careful examination, operative metaphors can control our thinking and our perceptions. This is dangerous ground for society—and especially our students.

Danesi reminds us how German philosopher Friedrich Nietzsche "came to see metaphor as humanity's greatest flaw, because of its subliminal power to persuade people into believing it on its own terms" (2004, 15).

Nietzsche certainly captured our susceptibility to metaphorical distortions in politics. Both Nietzsche and Kovecses (2002) speak to the manipulative power of metaphors to shape perceptions, especially what constitutes truth. Sure, we can use the initial metaphor to launch new thinking. But just as importantly, we must consider its tethers to the ordinary and uncorrelated aspects among the compared domains.

Let's reflect on the potential dangers of literary and historical metaphors, which may go unexamined in the classroom. For example, young people can be blinded to the horrors of war because of the way writers and political leaders romanticize military battles and heroism. Historian and war veteran Paul Fussell explores this practice in *The Great War and Modern Memory* (2000). He notes that British soldiers and the media used diction during World War I that was as heavy-handed as Arthurian legends. In the vernacular of the times, "horse" became "steed," "danger" became "peril," and dead soldiers were memorialized as "the fallen" (Fussell 2000, 21–22). Such persuasive metaphors, though certainly understandable during a period of patriotic fervor, glossed over the war's true brutality. In this conceptual world, King Arthur is noble and fictional, while having your body slashed in half by a machine gun is ugly and real. And, of course, "war is hell." World War I propaganda prompted many young men to volunteer for military service. The disillusionment and lost innocence that resulted are richly portrayed in Erich Maria Remarque's classic novel, *All Quiet on the Western Front*; many high schools and middle schools include the book in English and history curriculums, which presents a great opportunity for metaphorical exploration.

Metaphors That Obscure Meaning

Reverend Tom Berlin, mentioned in Chapter 3, is a big fan of metaphors. "The thing about metaphors is that they help us enter narrative," he says. "We could just state the metaphor or comparison straight out: 'Free will is like the bride asking her father to dance,' but what people really want to hear is the story. Without the story, the metaphor's effectiveness dims; people don't care."

At the same time, Berlin cites his concern that stories in sermons can sometimes become more powerful than the theology they are meant to illuminate. The metaphorical flourishes can be so compelling to listeners that the symbolism overshadows the message.

Berlin's caution applies to teaching. We can entertain and engage students with tales that elucidate strong metaphors and analogies, but do we also take the extra step to ensure that the intended comparison is clear in students' minds? And are we telling the story just to amuse students, or does it further our cause—the lesson's objectives? Teachers shouldn't do all the work for students. What's the payoff for them if we create the metaphor, then tell them a story that portrays it vividly and, finally, map all the connecting points between the concrete image and the abstract concept? Students need to learn how to identify those connections themselves. Otherwise, the learning won't be retained. The balance between overt explaining and guiding students' self-discovery is crucial for successful metaphor dissection.

Let's look at a few examples. In Chapter 7, we saw that graphic organizers can be powerful visual metaphors. Showing students how to use spatial and sequential models to construct and analyze metaphors is an excellent teaching strategy to deepen perception and reasoning skills. Yet depending on the way we structure knowledge within these visual frames, we can either clarify or distort thinking. Consider a hierarchical organizer such as the one in Figure 9.1. Charts such as this communicate a logic all their own. As you look at the graphic, you immediately get the sense of what's most important—lower levels are subservient to higher ones. Such graphics can serve a useful purpose for organizing and communicating function and responsibility. But if we teach students (overtly or passively) to accept the implied ideology without considering the implications, we miss the chance to enrich their metaphorical thinking. How? Look more closely at the conceptual underpinnings of this visual cue.

Consider how the diagram in Figure 9.1 places school administrators in the highest tier. What is the suggested value—responsibility? Power? Importance? This chart also positions teachers as just one of many branches within the school's structure. Is this an appropriate stature? What is the

Figure 9.1 Staff Chart of a Sample High School

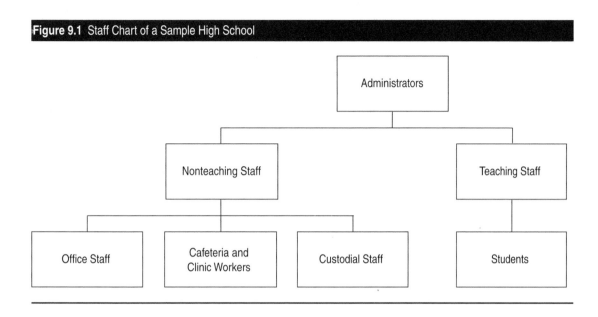

implication of the view? Is this the correct metaphor for the way we see schooling in our community? Maybe, maybe not.

What would we communicate to others if we switched two of the categories, students and administrators (see Figure 9.2)? What can we conclude about values from this second chart? What is the focus of this school organization, and how does it differ from the values expressed in the previous

Figure 9.2 Staff Chart of a Sample High School (Revised)

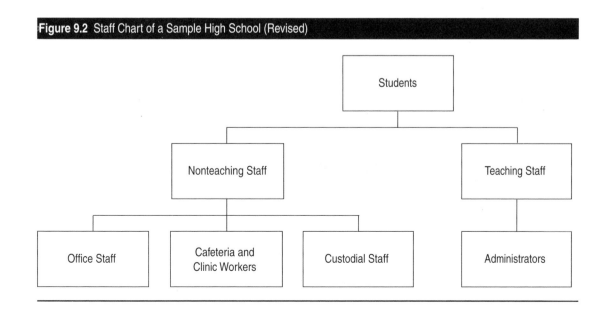

chart? Reassessing visual metaphors by changing categories or characteristics and watching what gets moved to the foreground and background in the hierarchy can lead to important conversations with students and colleagues.

Statistical Stealth Bombs

In addition to broadening the scope of metaphor as messenger, such critical analysis of metaphors improves students' media literacy skills. The rapid flow of information in our high-tech world has expanded resources and ways to learn. But the acceleration often surpasses our ability to prepare students for what they will find on the information superhighway. Do they know what to do with and how to interpret the data they discover? Classroom experience suggests that they do not. Metaphorical thinking improves their ability to synthesize and evaluate new concepts, such as understanding how people can manipulate data to promote their causes and prejudices.

To examine the possibilities for abuse and misinterpretation, imagine that you are making a choice of a college to attend and consider the data in Figure 9.3. Some of us look for the highest number of graduates and declare that the corresponding institution is the most successful institution: Orange College leads the pack with 3,189.

If we wanted to make the data even more vivid and comparative for visual learners, we could sell the point by reexpressing the data graphically (see Figure 9.4). A concrete thinker will search for the tallest bar and stop, satisfied with a simplistic interpretation of the data. Numbers are symbols of success, and if we're searching for a college, Orange College seems like the best choice to attend because it graduates more students than the other schools.

A mind that thinks metaphorically will rearrange statistics to consider other categories and meanings, however. Closer examination of the data and their patterns reveals flaws in our earlier thinking. The graphic portrayal in

Figure 9.3 Graduating Seniors of Four Institutions of Higher Learning			
College	**Number of Students**	**Graduating Seniors**	**Percent Graduating**
Apple University	10,500	2,009	19
Orange College	20,223	3,189	16
Banana Academy	5,600	1,405	25
Grape Institute	15,171	2,335	15

Figure 9.4 Graduating Seniors of Four Institutions of Higher Learning, Reexpressed Graphically

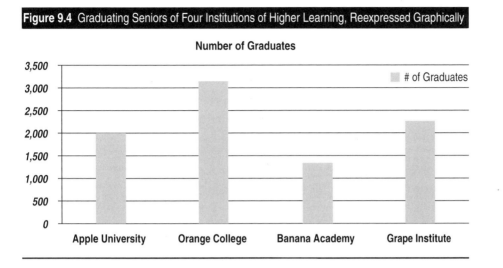

Figure 9.4 doesn't frame the information according to our needs; it only presents the number of graduates without analysis. If a graduation rate is a key factor in our choice of a college, then the percentage of graduates, not total number of graduates, would be a better predictor of our own success within that school community. In short, we need a different expression, a different metaphor (see Figure 9.5). When we look at the data presentation through the graphic organizer in Figure 9.5, we not only see that Orange College is one of the least appealing choices, but that Banana Academy does a significantly better job of matriculating students. With this metaphorical framework, we can make a better decision.

Figure 9.5 Percent of Graduating Seniors of Four Institutions of Higher Learning

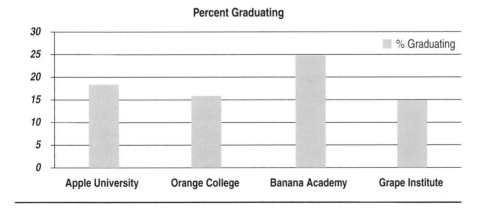

The lesson here is that metaphors are only as good as their analysis. Line graphs are useful for showing change over time, and bar graphs are better for expressing comparisons; any metaphor will not do. We must search for the correct metaphor and teach students to conduct due diligence too. Exploring the possibility that we have chosen the wrong metaphor is just as important as learning how to create a new one.

When teaching, we are careful to make sure students grasp our intentions. We double-check their understanding and application of metaphors and analogies. Otherwise, concrete interpretations may overshadow abstract reasoning because students are still learning how to comfortably navigate the conceptual realm.

Which Way Does Your Metaphor Flow?

The jobs of the future will demand greater synthesizing and interpretative skills than ever before, which means that our students must regularly practice constructing and critiquing symbolic representations of information. Let's explore another visual metaphor that makes this point more vivid.

Figure 9.6 uses machine sprockets to suggest the relationships among government regulation, free market enterprise, and economic innovation. The graphic seems to say that free market enterprise moves inversely to government regulation. And indeed, some economic and political theories teach

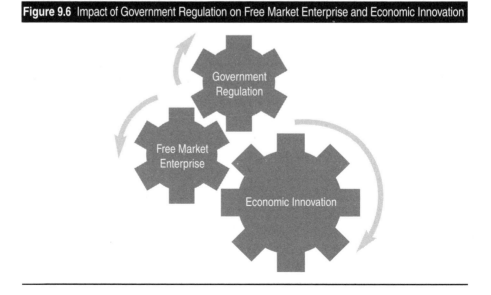

Figure 9.6 Impact of Government Regulation on Free Market Enterprise and Economic Innovation

this position: less regulation leads to greater capitalistic gains. In addition, the virtual metaphor states that the interaction of government regulation and free market enterprise impacts economic innovation, with economic innovation going the same direction as government regulation.

Are these relationships accurate? What if we step back and consider the metaphor from a different perspective? Some people view freedom as a catalyst for creativity. Free market enterprise stimulates economic innovation. The economic innovation wheel should turn the same direction as the free market enterprise wheel.

Here, however, we remember that necessity is the mother of invention. If the government imposes more regulation on small business owners, for example, that regulation may limit the growth and bottom line of those businesses. With increased regulation, then, do they have to innovate more in order to remain competitive? Maybe the virtual metaphor is accurate. Is this oversimplifying and not fully realistic about what really happens when the government clamps down on free market enterprise? Perhaps we shouldn't even use wheels in this graphic because we could claim that while the wheel is turning, some portion of it is rising up one side while another portion is falling down the other. Instead of wheels, maybe three engines should represent economic and government dynamos revving and idling as they interact with one another.

This is the moment of truth in our classrooms: Do we invite scrutiny of the metaphors we create and use? Do we teach students how to decode, test, repair, and reconstruct them? The full measure of a metaphor is revealed through discussion and analysis; an unexamined metaphor is incomplete learning.

Ripping Metaphors Apart at the Seams

One recognizes one's course by discovering the paths that stray from it.
—Albert Camus, 1942

Invite introspection when teaching metaphorical thinking. You and your students will benefit from the tougher tactics. To start, review the analogies and metaphors in your lesson plan or think back to examples that you have used recently. Now consider how you will guide students to question the comparisons:

Ladies and gentlemen, I claimed yesterday that the federal government's education policy paralyzed local officials' efforts to reduce class sizes in the elementary grades. I'd like you to work with a partner and explain the concept of "political paralysis." Then show me how the metaphor breaks down, given the characteristics of paralysis, federal policies, and local school reform practices.

Another time, you might want to let students practice with metaphorical expressions that have become clichés. These easy-to-challenge comparisons will provide safe harbor for novice sailors. Ask students to identify the intent of the metaphors and then to "rip them apart," exposing the limitations and distortions of each. Here's how Amy Benjamin does it in *Writing in the Content Areas*: "You can't think of feudalism as a ladder because you can climb up a ladder," she explains. "The feudal structure is more like sedimentary rock: what's on the bottom will always be on the bottom unless some cataclysmic event occurs" (2005, 80).

The metaphor-bashing list you provide to students might include the following:

- ⚡ Life is like an apple tree.
- ⚡ The structure of an essay is like a hamburger.
- ⚡ The stimulus and recovery package moved like an economic freight train.
- ⚡ The lawyer harvested the information from three witnesses.
- ⚡ The turmoil in the governor's mansion will bleed pressure off the other candidate.
- ⚡ She broke the glass ceiling.
- ⚡ Cancer is an unwelcome house guest.
- ⚡ Eyes are windows to the soul.
- ⚡ Urban renewal was the engine that powered the committee.
- ⚡ Their conversation was as risky as Russian roulette.
- ⚡ That remark was the tipping point in the debate.
- ⚡ The purpose of a neuron's myelin sheath is the same as the Police Department's motto: To serve and protect.

If some students struggle to break down the metaphors, provide models of deconstruction. Take, for example, "A classroom is like a beehive." Where does the simile sink?

- ⚡ Students have a variety of readiness levels and skill sets for completing tasks. Bees are more uniform.
- ⚡ Students don't respond blindly or purely to the pheromones of the queen bee.

⚡ Students are busier throughout the day and night than bees.

⚡ Students don't swarm when angered.

Test the Verb Strength

Did we *invade* the country, or did we *liberate* it? The choice of verbs determines perspective and colors social ethics. The verb frames our thinking, not to mention acceptance or censure by the world community. Word choice is more than a matter of semantics. It's a pivotal part of communication, especially if the verb serves as a metaphor.

Examining a simple statement such as the previous descriptions of a military conquest can lead to complex thinking if we give students the right metaphorical context. Here's a good activity to probe the predicate: Use sentence starters that describe concepts, events, or people mentioned in your studies. Ask students to change only the verb and explain how the reader or listener's interpretation of the topic would change as a result.

The senator *corralled* her constituents.
The senator *coddled* her constituents.
The senator *ignited* her constituents.
The senator *stonewalled* her constituents.
The senator *suckered* her constituents.
The senator *mollified* her constituents.
The senator *lifted* her constituents.

In each of the examples, a different metaphor is used as a verb. After students have discussed the meaning of each scenario as represented by the varied verbs, ask them to describe the possible impact. How might constituents feel as a result of the senator's actions, again depending on the portrayal represented through the changing verb? You might encourage students to dramatize the differences, using one of the physical experiences suggested in Chapter 6. Finally, through artwork or written reflection, ask students to describe an event in their own lives using three different verbs and explain how each scenario would change the result. Examples could include: eating dinner with family, asking someone for a favor, completing homework or chores, setting up an iPod playlist, fixing a toy, sending a text message, playing a sport, making breakfast, and answering a teacher's questions in class.

Turning Our Critical Eye to the Larger World

As students become more adept using metaphors and analogies to accelerate their learning, they will appreciate discovering how more accomplished thinkers use comparisons to clarify, limit, or obfuscate communication. You can give them a behind-the-scenes tour of your contemplations as a teacher. But in addition, encourage their interactions with other adults.

As part of my research for this book, I asked people in multiple professions to consider the role of metaphors in their work. One of the people I consulted was my dad, Paul Wormeli, executive director of the IJIS Institute, a consortium of law enforcement and information technology companies that provide leadership, training, and information sharing for justice and public safety officials around the world. Dad picked right up on the theme as he described the frequency of metaphor use in his job. But his insights about the emotional power of metaphors to inspire or dissuade gave both of us something to consider.

"Trying to keep up with the amount of information available today on crime and terrorism is like drinking out of a fire hose," he explained. Yet, almost as soon as he uttered that expression, he started analyzing the impact of the chosen metaphor.

"Of course, current metaphors can be a real impediment to discovery and thinking," he added. "Metaphors like the information fire hose can lead us to a sense of things being hopeless, when in fact they are not. Or they can oversimplify things so we don't recognize the complexity of the problem or the various ways to solve it. This can lead to inaction when action is most needed. If we teach people to go beyond the metaphor, they realize, 'Okay, that's the current picture, so what can we do about that?' With this thinking we open new vistas. We can't let the metaphor stop us. A metaphor like this may get people's attention, but it doesn't necessarily help people solve the problem."

So it seems that using metaphors is like buying computers. Almost as soon as we purchase a new computer and plug it in, we realize that it has become obsolete; knowledge and technology have moved on. With metaphors, we may identify what we think is a good one, only to later discover its limitations. This is not to say the metaphor isn't useful, just that it's prudent to be ever-critical of it as information changes.

Canadian Stephen Strauss (2009), writing for the *Globe and Mail*, widens metaphor vistas in his call for a new DNA metaphor:

I got fed up with the inexactitude of DNA metaphors and announced a contest. I asked readers to come up with an expression consisting of six words or fewer that captured the molecule's ability to replicate itself.

One reader, Trevor Spencer Rines, responded with: "DNA: the web which spins the spider. . . . If you look at a DNA molecule down its axis it looks like a spider web; then again, the idea of the molecule that unzips itself and puts itself back together reminded me of spiders consuming their own web and then respinning it."

Creating metaphors and then deconstructing and revising or replacing them is a very effective instructional strategy. We all progress in our thinking this way. So let's be intentional about following every declaration of a good metaphor with an equally interesting prompt to explain why it's *not* a good metaphor.

This back-and-forth analysis is especially helpful to students as they consider advanced applications of ideas and skills. What does the posted doubloon symbolize in Herman Melville's *Moby Dick*? What is he trying to say in the passage, and is he successful? If we follow that metaphor, do we arrive at the same place as the author? Is there a way to revise this metaphor and make it stronger?

I was reminded again of the recursive nature of metaphors and their power to shape and distort thinking while reading *Poetic Logic*. In it, Danesi recounts author Susan Sontag's analysis of cancer's evolution from a diagnosis to a medical metaphor for death: "'As long as a particular disease is treated as an evil, invincible predator, not just a disease, most people with cancer will indeed be demoralized by learning what disease they have'" (Sontag 1978, 7, quoted in Danesi 2004, 25). Can a metaphor kill? It's a troubling question, but one that we shouldn't be shy about raising with students as we probe the metaphors in our midst.

In another example, we often associate darkness with something bad, but we should ask of our students, is this wise? How does the "darkness is evil" perspective impact race relations among people of different skin colors? The oft-quoted phrase of civil rights leader Dr. Martin Luther King Jr., "Darkness cannot drive out darkness; only light can do that. Hate cannot drive out hate; only love can do that," provides perspective and a plan for action. It moves us in wonderful ways. There is poignancy in the old Chinese proverb used by John F. Kennedy and Adlai Stevenson, "It is better to light one candle than to curse the darkness." With both statements, however, we wonder what is lost because darkness is once again portrayed as something to be driven out and overcome. Could darkness be a place of comfort, safety, beauty, and perhaps in reflective, late-night conversations with close friends, illuminating?

One last quote from a wise advisor, Socrates, brings this metaphor analysis point home for many educators: "We are what we repeatedly do. Excellence, then, is a habit." Looking at our classrooms, daily metaphor deconstruction creates successful students, or put another way, tearing something down leads to stronger building.

Learning is a series of evolving metaphors, each one building perception and bringing us closer to truth. For some students who are in the early stages of development, metaphors that serve them now will no longer work as their thinking matures. That's cause for celebration but also reason to be cautious. It's important to teach through metaphors and help students develop their own cognitive comparisons, but we want to take a comprehensive approach. A crucial part of the process is teaching students how to critique metaphors, identifying their limitations and updating them when they no longer serve.

So keep clearing the cobwebs from the attic and dusting off the souvenirs in storage. New treasures will emerge.

10

Listening for Harmony and Discordant Sounds: Transcending Current Education Metaphors

E ducator and author Debbie Silver spent more than thirty years in the classroom, but she has never been comfortable coasting. Her reflection on the adaptive role of metaphors in teaching is an important reminder that we must keep sharpening our tools. Here's her story of transformation:

For many years my favorite metaphor for teaching was comparing the teacher's role to that of an orchestra conductor. A maestro must bring together a mix of musicians, just as the teacher seeks to blend students who manifest a wide range of resonance and distinctiveness. Both conductor and teacher seek to create a melodic, rhythmic ebb and flow among their group members. The orchestra leader must be knowledgeable about all the instruments in play; a teacher must be well-informed about the full range of student personalities, competencies, and experiences. Both maestro and master teacher encourage individuals to make their own contributions to the group's symphony.

As I made this analogy I pictured a teacher on a riser, baton in hand, gently guiding discussions and interactions among students. She waves her hands to draw learners in and gently move them away toward independent pursuits. I postulated that the roles of conductor and teacher are similar because both require a clear vision of the desired final outcome along with an ability to break down the larger product into achievable increments. The conductor and teacher are likely to be more successful if they manifest a passion for what they do, an ability to improve through reflective practice, and a belief that effective rehearsal enhances performance. Yes, I was quite satisfied with my model and used it extensively to describe what teaching was like.

There are, of course, obvious differences between conductors and teachers. The orchestra leader usually has a hand in selecting his members. Most often he has the power to permanently remove an undesirable or underperforming member from the group. His focus is on a single or set of performances that are melodic, syncopated, and as close to perfection as humanly possible.

Upon deeper examination, I realized how flawed this particular metaphor is for teaching. Effective teachers are not paragons who stand before self-selected participants anxious to follow their every command. Exemplary teachers involve their students in decision making, goal setting, procedures, and power sharing. They spend most of their time not in front of the class but on the sidelines as coaches and advocates.

Whereas the maestro is fixated on a final performance, consummate educators focus on individual process and progress. Students are not just standard instruments—they are evolving individuals who are a unique blend of special skills, talents, experiences, and interests. Life in the classroom is not so much about a single harmonious pursuit as it is a joyful array of disjointed starts and stops and all manner of organized chaos. Unlike the orchestra leader's objective of having his performers reach their peak moment simultaneously in concert, teachers seek to help students find their own rhythms and strengths on their own timetables. Educators should not be asked to prepare students for the "one shot" performance piece, but rather prepare them to become growing lifelong learners.

My earlier metaphor limited my vision of my role as a teacher. It supported a product-oriented approach to teaching as opposed to a process-centered student advocacy role. The original metaphor was based on extrinsic motivation rather than the intrinsic motivation sought by truly exceptional teachers. To make my teaching better, I had to change my metaphor. I am still trying to create a comparison that aptly reflects my desire to come down off that riser and actively involve my students in the whole process of learning. Perhaps our policy makers need to consider a new metaphor, too.

Silver sets a good example for introspection: Are we open to examining our teaching from multiple perspectives, even if the self-analysis suggests that our operative metaphors aren't working as well as we once thought? If we are to evolve as a profession and thereby as a society, we must be willing to reconsider the metaphors that form and bind our instruction.

Redefining Our Roles

If we accept the tenet that perception is reality, it's not a far leap to also accept the premise that metaphors can be manipulated and, in turn, manipulate us—altering truth along the way. Steven Pinker (2007) claims that truth is a competition among metaphors. If this is accurate, then the big question is, Whose metaphor will we accept as fact? Will it be one that we generate ourselves, or will we borrow someone else's view? Teachers must be willing to revise their thinking in light of new evidence and to remain vigilant against blind acceptance of stated truth—the perceived metaphor of the time.

We are immersed in metaphors that shape our thinking and actions on both micro and macro scales. Some of these principles are so embedded in our culture that we never question them:

⚡ Why do we teach all students through grade 12, not just the ones easiest to teach and who want to be there?

⚡ Why do we have grade levels?

⚡ Is our classroom set up for teachers or for students?

⚡ Whose voice isn't heard in our deliberations?

⚡ How are our current structures limiting us?

⚡ Does our master schedule support best instructional practices, or have we sacrificed best practices for the sake of the master schedule?

⚡ Why do we grade students, and are we achieving that purpose?

⚡ What is the role of homework?

⚡ Does it matter whether every student demonstrates mastery of the same standard on the same day of the year, or is it more important that they learn the material well, even if it takes longer?

⚡ Are there other school calendars that might work better for our students?

⚡ Does our use of technology advance student learning?

⚡ What do I need to unlearn this year to improve my instruction?

⚡ Where in my lesson plans do I see evidence of my expertise in cognitive science and the unique nature of students at this age?

⚡ How does assessment inform my practice?

⚡ Is our school's culture toxic (e.g., unhealthy for growth and for freedom to learn and work)?

⚡ Is my goal that my students will get only to my level of competence
    with this material, or is my goal that they will surpass me?

⚡ Does this assignment really advance students in their learning or
    does it keep them at stasis?

Upsetting the Apple Cart

When I taught middle school social studies, the curriculum covered the history of the United States from Reconstruction through modern times. I would march my students chapter by chapter chronologically through the curriculum all year long and finally arrive at World War II just before the last three weeks of school in June. More than 50 years in less than a month, just when students pay the least amount of attention? This was nuts! I never did justice to that portion of our studies.

So one year I taught anti-chronologically: I started with the modern age and worked backwards to Reconstruction. It worked. Students were flexible and certainly more interested. They relished looking at history in terms of patterns, themes, and causes and consequences, not just a linear sequence of meaningless events and people. I never taught history the conventional way again.

Or consider the traditional way of dealing with students who persistently misbehave. We give them after-school detentions, suspend them from school, or put them in self-contained classrooms with other chronically defiant youths. But teachers who carefully examine the metaphor of corrections—misbehavior must be contained—soon realize that this singular and simplistic response rarely works. Changing behavior requires ongoing interventions that target a variety of factors that cause children to act out in school. So instead of repeating patterns of failure, reflective teachers choose a different metaphor: a *systems* response. They might try some of the following interventions:

⚡ Provide a single adult advocate who meets with the errant student
    every day.

⚡ Meet with the parents and collaborate about ways to reinforce consistent messages about personal responsibility at home and school.

⚡ Suggest changes to the student's sleep schedule.

⚡ Place the student in a looped class in which the teacher stays with
    the same group for more than a year.

⚡ Change the student's class schedule so that more-demanding
    courses come after 10 a.m., when the student is more likely to be
    awake and engaged.

⚡ Suggest changes to the student's diet and ensure that he or she gets regular exercise.

⚡ Facilitate a medical check-up to see if there are physiological concerns.

⚡ Screen the student for any kind of learning challenges.

⚡ Adjust instructional approaches.

⚡ Collaborate with the student's pastor/rabbi/sports coach.

⚡ Seek counseling for the student and his family.

⚡ Make sure the student has glasses and other tools of learning, if needed.

⚡ Involve local social workers, police officers, and school psychologists, as warranted.

Changing the metaphor of discipline—recognizing the multidimensions of misbehavior—creates the opportunity for success. It's similar to how we recover from an injury. We usually take some kind of medical treatment, and we also rest, eat properly, undergo therapy, exercise, take extra time, move slowly at first but faster later, and even get support from family and friends. We don't rely on just one of these factors in order to heal; we do several in tandem. The healing response dovetails with the discipline response, and we find a more constructive course of action. Instead of framing behavioral digressions as a personal affront that justifies our anger toward students, we see their misbehaviors as calls for healing things that hurt.

Take a look at some of the common metaphors of our teaching profession in Figure 10.1 and see if they still serve.

You and your colleagues may find that some of these frames still work, that some are more limited, and that some of them never worked. The task then is two-fold. First, be aware of current metaphors that shape our thinking. Second, question those metaphors and, if you can't justify their usefulness, find new or amended metaphors that lead to better student learning.

Consider the metaphorical framework for special education. How does it change our thinking and our instruction if we define the "L.D." in "L.D. student" as "learns differently" instead of "learning disabled"? Our attitude and actions change significantly with such a mind-set: Tamara, in my third-period class, isn't disabled. Instead, my regular instructional approach doesn't meet her needs because she learns differently. I either must redesign the lesson or develop alternate approaches so she can progress as well as others. This is a completely different mind-set (metaphor). Adopting it improves Tamara's success in school.

Bill Ivey, an innovative educator at Stoneleigh-Burnham school in Greenfield, Massachusetts, reminded me of another common education

---

Figure 10.1 Common Metaphor Frames for Teaching

The child as a blank slate	Master schedule
Benchmarks and standards	Study hall
No child left behind	Failure as an option
Factory model of schooling	Mission
Cultural literacy	Accelerated
Active learning	Gifted
Teacher as police officer	Grading curve
Teams and pods	Parallel curriculum
We mold lives	Open classroom
Children are clay	Scaffolding
Teacher as gatekeeper	Tiering
Bag of tricks	Inclusion
Suspend students	Accountability
Locus of control	High-stakes
Covering the curriculum	Brain-based
Ivory tower	Grades are affirmation
Progressive	Learning disabled
School system	Scratch paper
Top-down mandates	Child-centered
Teacher as coach	Steering committee
Jigsaw	Mainstream
Chunking learning	Least restrictive environment
Weighted grades	Achievement gap
School climate	Time out
Computer lab	Accommodation
Core subjects	Norm vs. individualization
Subject integration	Hall duty (opportunity?)
Block schedule	Whole language

---

metaphor that begs to be reconsidered. He first questioned the metaphor, and then provided a beautiful alternative:

> In the movie Parenthood, *Rick Moranis is talking to Steve Martin about children and learning, and says, "Our children are more capable of absorbing information than we are, yet we insist on treating them like adorable little morons . . . They're like sponges, Gil, just waiting to absorb." Though well-meaning, I would argue this metaphor is at the root of much of what is wrong with our educational system today. First, the assumption that the older we get, the less capable we are of acquiring information undermines the whole concept of lifelong learning. Second, all too often we treat our children like adorable little morons, assuming they need more help from us than they truly do. Third, and most pernicious, the idea of children being sponges ready to absorb*

information sets up the expectation that the information must be pro-
vided to them rather than sought by them. Prescribed curricula, mas-
sively detailed frameworks and standards, and the idea that school is
about teachers teaching rather than students learning, all spring from
this perspective. What if children were like whales, taking in massive
amounts of information, straining out what is extraneous, and making
good use of what remains?

"What if . . .?" Bill asks. That's a very effective start for any metaphor revision. To bring this closer to our daily classroom practices, let's consider a
metaphor that can have serious consequences if we never question it.
Grading: "What if we're doing it incorrectly?"

Look at one aspect of standards-based (outcomes-based) education.
Many teachers struggle with rounding zeroes on the 100-point grading scale
to 50 or higher. They think, "I'm not giving students something for having
done nothing. That's not truthful, nor does it prepare students for the world
beyond school." These teachers are mired in the metaphor that grades are
compensation. They will never see the fallacy of their response as long as
they hold on to that belief.

Grades are not intended to be compensation, affirmation, or validation,
which are all promoted with statements from teachers such as, "You can get
an A on this project if you . . ." and "You earned a B on the test." Instead,
grades are supposed to be forms of *communication*. They are an accurate
report of what students know and are able to do, nothing else. When they are
used for other purposes, they are no longer useful.

The accuracy part is crucial. If anything distorts the report of what students know, we should remove it from our grading practices. In the case of
zeroes on the 100-point scale, we realize that all letter grades should have
equal influence on the overall calculation of the grade. If we give one of the
letter grades a 60-point influence (scoring anywhere from 0 to 59 in many
schools constitutes an F grade) when each of the other grades—A, B, C, and
D—has only a 10- or 11-point influence on the 100-point scale, we skew the
accuracy of the report of what students know and are able to do regarding
standards or outcomes.

If we accept the new metaphor of grades as communication, not compensation, we can move the zero to a 60 without worry, realizing that the
grade still indicates an F, or "no evidence of learning." We just made the F
recoverable instead of hopeless, mathematically justified rather than suspect.
This is a very contentious issue for many educators, of course, but the first
place to look as we sort through any educational issue is the underlying

metaphor. In this case, with zeroes turning into sixties, the metaphor upon which we act can make or break whole school careers because of grade point averages that allow or disallow people to get into colleges of their choice. Metaphors are not abstractions only to be considered in philosophy class. They have direct impact on our daily lives.

Look at the previous list of education metaphors one more time. Choose one of these or another one that is part of the culture of your school and rip it apart. What is the implied comparison, and what are the limitations of the metaphor? Is another metaphor needed in order to progress? Can we do something else besides hang students in mid-air (*suspend*)? Is it a hall *connection time* or a hall *duty*? What are we *steering* on that committee, and should we be doing so? Are we really "whole" in our *whole language* program? When is learning anything but *active*? What does it mean to *accelerate* students or the curriculum, and is faster better? Is our classroom technology a *learning tool* or a *time-sucking device*? Are we *fenced in* by *high stakes*? Do we need more *data analysis* or *data synthesis*? Is the curriculum *parallel* or *overlaid*? Do we have a curriculum *map*, *encyclopedia*, or *poker game*?

An early reviewer of my book manuscript reinforced the importance of looking at education through multiple lenses. "Several years ago, I had the good fortune to work for a principal who was able to frame all our initiatives about change in powerful metaphors," she said. "I realized then that this visualization was incredibly important for me to get on board with change. I was totally a 'good soldier' ready to do whatever was expected if I got the metaphor.

"There was a real lesson for me in this aspect of leadership. The change initiative often feels really abstract or really far from where we are now, but a good metaphor allows me to see relationships and structure and, often, the emotion of why/how/what the change will be."

Personal Metaphor Wrestling

Choosing the right metaphors opens doors. Never questioning them keeps us cloistered and unaware—not the best stimulation for teaching excellence. With all learning, the deepest thinking and best decisions come as we wrestle with ideas and publicly defend our positions. We need to discuss our conceptual frameworks frequently. It's as simple as asking colleagues, "What's the metaphor we're using here, and does it work for us?"

Let me offer my own current metaphor wrestling:

1. *Schools shouldn't be places of stability. Instead, they should be places of compelling disequilibrium.* Author and educator Margaret Wheatley (2006) reminds us that equilibrium is a system at rest: Stasis doesn't require anything. It doesn't produce anything; it's effectively inert. This is not what schools aspire to be. Calm waters can endanger sailors by lulling them into complacency. When a sailboat rides up on whitecaps, the boat leaning heavily under full sail, the crew can fully practice the skills of navigation. That's what we need in education—something that keeps us slightly off center keel, forcing us to bring the rocking boat back into balance until the next storm.

2. *Teachers are not distributors of knowledge, nor are we knowledge fountains from which students drink.* If we're doing our jobs well, the next generation will inspire us, challenge us, change us, and surpass us. Imagine if we limited our students to our limited imaginations; society would stagnate. The goal should be to help students write a better paragraph, take math ideas further, and think of greater possibilities. We are helpful interpreters and fortunate facilitators, but the genius of our students must be set free.

3. *Teaching is not telling*, yet many teachers think students learn content merely by hearing the descriptions. Mark Twain wisely cautioned, "If teaching were telling, we'd all be so smart we couldn't stand ourselves." It's time to evolve beyond lecture as the prime teaching tool.

4. *Teaching is not a 50-50 partnership with students*, such as when some teachers declare, "Students have to meet me halfway." This is a highly inappropriate ratio. Most students do not have the maturity or training to be given such influence over their learning. A student who exclaims, "I don't care if I get an F on my test. School sucks!" shouldn't be put in charge of his destiny. For successful teachers, the responsibility is closer to a 70-30 ratio. We get the horse to water, and we do everything we can to make it thirsty.

5. *Textbooks are not the curriculum*; they are a resource. Many educators know this intellectually but they don't act on it. They still go to the next page of the textbook because it's the next page of the textbook, not because it serves their students. We should go to page 73 or page 173 or no textbook page at all, depending on the needs of our students.

6. *P.E. and the arts are not sacrificial lambs upon the altar of standardized test preparation.* In fact, it is often these two areas that give what we do in other classes dimension and meaning. I've lost count of the

number of research studies indicating how physical education and the arts positively influence performance in other content courses. It's time we took steps to protect these courses with the same fervor that we use to protect math and reading.

7. *"Students are apathetic sloths" is not a tenable attitude of professional educators.* If a student manifests the characteristics of laziness, there is always something else going on that we can't see. Unless disturbed by one of those rare physiological imbalances, no one wakes up in the morning and declares that she wants to be a loser, unproductive, or dead wood in the classroom. Today's students are participating in life on multiple levels, dealing with more information and producing more than ever before, but classrooms based on yesterday's perceptions may not give them a chance to show it.

8. *Teaching is not a "gotcha" enterprise.* Some teachers think their job is done when they catch students making mistakes. Instead, our focus should be increasing students' readiness and confidence to succeed, not documenting their deficiencies. Students are watching us, hoping the world really is compassionate, yet fearing that it's not safe or supportive. We can assure them that the world is demanding yet compassionate and, more important, that they have the tools to deal with it. Teamwork is valued in every aspect of society, so why aren't we showing students how they can contribute individually and collectively? Entrepreneurship, science exploration, and solving global problems such as malnutrition require risk taking and usually involve some failures before success. Students need practice with life's ebb and flow and some assurance that they have the skills to navigate the shifting currents.

9. *The teacher shouldn't be the processor of knowledge.* If a student asks a question and the teacher responds to it by stating the correct answer and asking the student follow-up questions, the teacher learns a lot. But something's wrong with this picture; the teacher already knows the material. Whoever is responding to students is doing the majority of the learning. Let's make sure it's students responding to students: teachers are redirectors.

10. *School shouldn't be about the information presented to students; it should reflect what students carry forward after learning.* Principals, school boards, state/provincial governments, legislators, communities, and business leaders do not care as much about what we're teaching as what our students learn. We should stop rallying our energy and politics around the inputs and focus on the outputs. The

best evidence of a teacher's, school's, or district's effectiveness is the consistent and creative application of knowledge that students gained while they were there.

The Reality and Inspiration of Metaphors

Steven Pinker (2007) writes about Judge Michael Boudin, former Chief Judge of the United States Court of Appeals for the First Circuit, who argues that "judges can be illicitly affected by metaphors such as the 'fruit of the poisonous tree' (illegally obtained evidence), the 'wall of separation between church and state,' and 'bottleneck monopolies' (companies that control a distribution channel such as a power grid or realty listing service)"(245). Recognizing this influence, judges spend considerable time vetting multiple "truths," looking for facts, causation, relationships, comparisons, and credence in their application of justice. They go out of their way to remain neutral, but in the end, they are just like the rest of us—influenced by the metaphors in play.

If the judicial system is constrained by conventional metaphors, it's just a short leap to consider the barriers we impose on thinking in education with our metaphors. We should be fighting for facts, relationships, comparisons, and credence just as much as judges do, and that comes with critical analysis and purposeful use of metaphors and analogies.

In addition to its connections to theology, the word *epiphany* refers to "a sudden, intuitive perception of or insight into the reality or essential meaning of something, usually initiated by some simple, homely, or commonplace occurrence or experience" (*Dictionary.com Unabridged* 2009). This definition offers a fitting description of metaphors and analogies that we can use to teach any subject. Metaphorical thinking often evokes aha! moments of insight into the "essential meaning of something," and what's particularly apt is the recognition that these moments of insight are often the result of connections with "simple, homely, or commonplace" occurrences or experiences. Scientists refer to the moon, for example, as earth's attic (*Talk of the Nation: Science Friday* 2009). This is because at least 1 percent or more of the moon's mass is made of rocks and other debris thrown off our planet by volcanic events and the impact of comets hitting the earth throughout its geologic history. In fact, scientists claim that, at some point, we'll find evidence of dinosaur bones on the moon because of the comet that crashed into the earth 65,000,000 years ago. Because an attic is a repository of our cultural/historical material, the Smithsonian Institution in Washington, D.C., is known as "The Nation's Attic." For most of us, the notion of something "up there" storing elements from "down here," such as an attic in a house, explains why we find pieces of earth, and even Venus and Mars, on the moon. We connected new learning to something familiar.

This book makes the point that successful students and teachers reexpress abstract concepts by making connections to familiar terms. The student Pete's dog guarding the front porch, the metaphor for America's behavior during war that opens Chapter 1, is one example of how we can use metaphorical thinking to make sense of new information. This may be metaphor's great power: the tools for effective instruction are literally all around us, ready to be perceived. But we must act purposefully to ensure that our classrooms provide regular and varied opportunities for students to harness the power.

Looking back over the instruction in my classroom since first becoming a teacher in the early 1980s, I realize that the most effective lessons, the experiences students cite years later, involved some kind of reinterpretation of content—a metaphor or analogy. Much of my differentiated instruction, for example, involved adaptations that made the curriculum individually meaningful to diverse students. As a result, all of my students were more successful on their assessments. The metaphorical thinking that enabled our curricular dexterity improved my teaching and my students' learning.

Certainly, understanding how we learn and communicate through metaphors and analogies is a cornerstone for the critical-thinking foundations we seek to build in students. Moving metaphors from incidental use to instructional prime time, we can make constructive comparisons an overt focus of our planning and our lesson and assessment design. Seriously, let's start asking ourselves and our colleagues such profession-stretching questions as:

"What's your underlying metaphor in the lesson?"

"Can you think of how this same principle could be expressed in terms of a topic that is more relevant to students' lives?"

"How does this operative metaphor limit us or our thinking?"

"What model would best portray this concept we're teaching today?"

"Look around this classroom. What could we use to demonstrate the principle we're teaching?"

"How did thinking metaphorically in your planning and instruction reveal something about the topic or your teaching that you hadn't seen before?"

As Plato suggested, we should be the ones who show students and each other that the flickering shadows on the back wall of the cavern are not all there is to reality. Recognizing and moving beyond our current metaphors may be the best gift we provide to the next generation. And their enthusiastic response, "Oh, now I get it!" is music to a teacher's ears.

Metaphorical Terms and Devices

Allegory: The communication of something about life through symbolic figures and events, such as in narrative; an extended metaphor that uses a story to make a point.

Analogy: Recognition that the relationship between two things is similar to the relationship between two other things ("flurries" is to "blizzard" as "candlelight" is to "klieg light"[increasing intensity]); making an inference of similarity, or noting the correspondence, between two things based on shared characteristics, such as describing how the structure of an essay is like that of a sandwich.

Anthropomorphism: The attribution of human characteristics to something that is not human, such as "shouldering a burden, going belly up, cups have lips, combs teeth, and fixtures knuckles" (Danesi 2004, 73).

Antithesis: The direct opposite of something; the contrasting of ideas "by means of parallel arrangements of words, clauses, or sentences (as in . . . 'they promoted freedom and provided slavery'")" (Merriam-Webster 2004, 56).

Conceit: A specific, innovative thought; an elaborate metaphor.

Euphemism: The substitution of something agreeable or tolerable to the listener or reader when communicating an idea or message that is not as agreeable or tolerable, such as telling students they have "a wonderful opportunity to demonstrate their advanced knowledge" when we announce that they will have a test on Friday.

Hyperbole: An exaggeration, such as, "It was a mountain of food!"

Idioms: A statement of two or more words that is uniquely understood by the participants in a conversation. The general meaning of the statement cannot be discerned from the literal meaning or application of the words involved, such as when describing a classroom as a "three-ring circus" or when describing a large work project as "having my job cut out for me." Interestingly, Sam Glucksberg (2001) notes while analyzing the idiom "kick the bucket" that we learn idioms whole, but we can be flexible in their applications and structures as long as we have key anchor points in the mapping. For example, we can say "kick the proverbial bucket"; "he'll be kicking the bucket soon"; or "he didn't kick the bucket, he nicked it slightly."

Irony: A surprise or unexpected outcome, sequence, or thought; "the use of words to express something other than the opposite of the literal meaning" (Merriam-Webster 2004, 662). Examples: "The silence was deafening." "The sea snake drowned." "The economic advisor filed for bankruptcy."

> I call architecture frozen music.
> —Johann Wolfgang von Goethe, 1829

Metaphor: A term or description that substitutes "one kind of object or idea . . . in place of another to suggest a likeness or analogy between them" (Merriam-Webster 2004, 780); a symbol.

Metonymy: The use of part of a topic to reference or stand for that topic. Kovecses says, "Conceptually, it can be defined as the process of using a part of a domain to represent the whole domain, or aspects of a domain to implicate either the whole domain or subsections of it . . . [such as] 'I've got a new set of wheels,' 'We need new blood in this organization,' 'Get your butt over here!' 'The Milwaukee Brewers need a stronger arm in right field' (2002, 74–75).

Onomatopoeia: Naming something based on the sound associated with it, such as, "The horses clopped along the cobblestone street." We recognize that horse hooves make the sound of "clop, clop, clop" when walking on such surfaces.

Oxymoron: A label, phrase, or statement made of seemingly contradictory or incongruous words, such as, "differentiated standardization" or "standardized differentiation."

Parable: An extended metaphor told as a small story, usually to illustrate a moral.

Paradox: A statement or situation in which elements seem to contradict common sense or what is currently accepted as truth. An example would be the Grandfather Paradox in time travel theories; we find it impossible to go back through a time machine to kill our grandfather before he married our grandmother and gave birth to our mother who in turn gave birth to us. If we were never born, how do we account for the role we played in the death of our grandparent? A paradox becomes metaphorical when we compare one paradox with another: "Creating a physically invisible plane is like pushing a camel through the eye of a needle."

Personification: Giving human qualities to inanimate objects. "The clock ticked loudly, each second-hand sweep scolding me like a schoolmaster and reminding me that I would never finish the exam in the allotted time."

Predicative metaphor: The use of specific verbs to connote something other than literally what they state, such as, "John *faced* reality," "When she became the chief executive officer, she *shattered* the glass ceiling," or "His hopes were *crushed* when he opened the socks for a birthday present."

Rhetorical question: An inquiry asked just to get listeners to think further about a topic but without the expectation of a definite response: "Let's consider the possibility—could this disease become the next Ebola virus?"

Simile: A comparison between two unlike objects or ideas using *like* or *as* in the comparison: "His speech was like frost: we shivered slightly and tried to preserve the ebbing warmth."

Symbol: An object, sign, character, act, or a small graphic that represents something else. For example, + represents addition. While an abstract symbol can represent a real object, such as the figure of a woman on the women's washroom door, a symbol can also represent something abstract, such as the symbol ☮, which represents peace. An act can also be a symbol for an abstract idea. For instance, a large gathering of voters for a political candidate is a symbol of animosity toward the current leader.

Synecdoche: A type of metonymy in which a specific part of something is used to refer to that larger something, such as "Many hands cleaned the park on Saturday," where hands are an actual part of the people who cleaned the park. Metonymy can also include those phrases where the smaller item of reference is only associated with the larger category, but is not literally a part of it. In the example "The White House blocked the tax reforms," the White House refers to the president and his advisers, but it is not literally a part of any of the bodies of those people.

Synectics: "The joining together of different and apparently irrelevant elements," or put more simply, "making the familiar strange" (Gordon 1971, 35). Students use synectics when they describe a topic in terms of a completely unrelated category, such as listing four connections between parts of speech and a coral reef or between the settlement of a continent and the patterns of insect behavior. In health class, the student might compare a part of the human body with a sport: "The endocrine system is like playing zones in basketball because each player or gland is responsible for his or her area of the game (body)."

Note: All definitions, except where noted, were created by the author or modified from examples found in *Merriam-Webster's Collegiate Dictionary*, 11th edition, 2004.

In the Classroom: Creative Examples of Metaphors from Teachers

As I was researching and writing this book, I was fortunate to learn from teachers around the world who use metaphors to convey topics across the curriculum. As catalysts for our divergent thinking, I offer the following examples.

English

An epic is a baseball game: the hero starts at home, needs to leave for a quest, encounters trials along the way that try to prevent him from his ultimate goal: returning home.

Patterns in literature, such as a plot structure, are there to make stories more understandable. Every new story is like getting a new car: you know that the headlights turn on somehow, the windshield wipers have a switch, etc. You just have to find it in the new car, the story. We continue to look for the "switches" that we know should be somewhere in the story.

—Karen Molter

Lately, the ongoing metaphor has been between making a cake and writing and revising final drafts. We talk a lot about the importance of

all the ingredients in a "good" piece of writing, just like cake . . . if you miss something it's just not the same. As far as revision goes, they struggle with adding inside their writing rather than just to the end (or on top). Once you bake the cake . . . pass it in for final grade . . . you can no longer add ingredients. You have to make sure you have them all in there before you hit the oven, and I'm the oven. They like the egg analogy the best: I tell them that once I bake the cake, it might look great, but I know I forgot the eggs and it's going to taste terrible. So, I take the eggs and crack them open and smear them all over the cake. Then I'm done. Right?

They understand how that doesn't work. We do a little frosting work. Especially with PowerPoint presentations . . . looking pretty on the outside still doesn't make a cake. If you are missing ingredients, it won't taste good or be good. They have had fun tying specific ingredients to specific writing skills . . . The sugar is the description, the flour is the transition and fluency that ties everything together. Good vocabulary is the egg, making it rich and fluffy.

—Trisha Fogarty

My tenth graders were struggling to understand essays and the ins and outs of rhetoric. They knew very little about writing, but they knew a lot about court and trials, so I helped them make the connection between the way lawyers present arguments and rhetorical arguments. The most helpful part of the analogy was connecting the idea that evidence has to be presented. Saying something doesn't make it so. This helped them understand the importance of using examples to flesh out their rhetorical arguments.

—Amy Bailey

When teaching writing with middle school students, especially essay writing, I want students to really develop their idea first, and elaborate a lot, before worrying about structure. My former coteacher, Jane Willis, came up with the metaphor of "rolling out" your idea like pie dough. You roll it because the dough has to completely cover the pan. Then later, you trim it to fit the shape of the pan perfectly. The year we cotaught, she actually brought in pie dough and a rolling pin and the students watched while she rolled it out, stretched it over the tin, then trimmed it down, linking it to the writing process. I have used the metaphor ever since.

—Ariel Sacks

I have a metaphor I use a lot called the helicopter. I started out using it just for reading, specifically, when talking about the different strategies used for different types of texts and purposes. Sometimes in research, for example, we need to move fast over a lot of terrain and our chopper is high in the air. When we see something of interest, from scanning a list of hits or a table of contents, we descend closer to the text. When we at last find a place where we want to touch ground, we are reading slowly and carefully. We can even get out of the helicopter and walk on the ground to look for evidence. But as soon as we're done, we can get back into it, move to any height and speed over the terrain. This has been a really helpful concept for a lot of my students, and I think I have some end-of-course "position papers" from the last crop of night school students that testify to this.

This also works with writing: sometimes we need to give a reader the big picture, like near the top of an expository piece on Darfur with a history of the region and the conflict. But when we get to important points, we need to slow down and zoom in.

—Emmet Rosenfeld

My mom actually taught me a wonderful metaphor activity to illustrate the parts of speech. This "House of Grammar" idea works like this:

Each of the eight parts correlates to a part of the structure of a house. The verb is the foundation of the house, as it is what holds a sentence together—the most important word in the sentence, the word that a sentence must have to be a sentence—as a foundation is needed to support a house. Next comes the frame of the house—the noun. It is the "biggest" part of the house, as nouns are frequent and many. The adjectives are the "decorations" on the house—curtains on the windows, planter boxes on the window frames, fancy doors . . . The adverbs are the steps leading to the house, connected to the foundation (the verb). The conjunction is the gutter that runs along the top of the house—the "connector" between the frame and the roof. Pronouns are represented by the roof—they "cover" for the nouns. Prepositions are "chains" of smoke puffs coming out of the chimney—they lead phrases, never standing alone. Finally, interjections are "bursts" of flowers in the front yard.

I have the kids draw the houses with the parts labeled. Every year they amaze me with their creativity and higher level applications. Many take this idea and apply it to things like people, cars, rockets, and sports fields.

—Jeanne White

Teacher Bill Ivey, at Stoneleigh-Burnham School, introduced his poetry unit by asking students to incorporate a major component of poetry—metaphors—in order to describe poetry. His students showed potential for their later development early in the process:

Poetry is the cloud in the sky. We can't guess a cloud's shape, color, or the weather that the cloud will make. Sometimes the cloud covers the sky, but sometimes it shows all the sky.

—Ashley Chung

Poetry is a face, which is always changing its expression.

—Jessie Bartolotta

Poetry is a black hole that you fall in and can't get out of.

—Alyssa Cote

Poetry is the breaking point from reality. It tips the meanings, causing a downpour of ideas waiting for questioning. The poet reveals each thought through the piece of paper which speaks not on its own, but with beautiful assistance.

—Erin Moore

Poetry is a form of emotions. You don't need to share it on your body, write it out, read it, hear it; it is like a rainbow. First it rains and then out comes the rainbow. First you feel your emotions, then your pen hits the paper like sparks and away you write.

—Alissa Ames

Grammar and Math

I have tried to help kids understand some of the English concepts by using math because I often get honors-level students who are more inclined this way. Math sentences can help them visualize language sentences.

To explain subordination and coordination of ideas in sentences I encourage the students to think of coordinating conjunctions as an equal sign (=) and that the ideas on either side of the coordinator (and, but, or) are essentially equal in weight. In subordinating clauses I ask the students to consider the subordination like a greater-than, less-than sign

*(< >) and that the subordinator (which, although, since, etc.)
expresses an idea that is either above, below, or in some way dependent
on the other main clause.*

*For parallel structure in sentences I remind them what parallel
lines are in math class—lines that run side by side. I show them parallel structure by lining up the listed phrases/items on the board in parallel form so the students can see that each part needs to be expressed in a
similar manner.*

*I also use fractals to help explain microcosm and universal ideas.
The idea of fractals is that there are repeated shapes and patterns
throughout the universe—another compelling idea that impacts mathematical, humanitarian, and spiritual thought—not to mention driving
the underlying algorithms that make many of our computers store
large amounts of digital images. And, as further evidence, we are truly
part of one thing.*

*In my classroom I have a visual I asked my husband to create for
me. It shows two mirrors, one intact and one broken. The intact mirror
represents the experiences of all of humanity. I tell the students that we
can all see all of us in the classroom in the intact mirror. The broken mirror pieces each represent a single individual's experience. But, I point out,
we can also see all of us in the small broken piece because when we read
(or write) a well-written experience, we can see ourselves in it too
because we can see the element of universal experience—those things we
all share because we are human. That seems to make sense to them and
they find the visual compelling, often asking about it before I get to it.*

—Mary Tedrow

History

*The Townshend Acts were proposed by a politician in England nick-
named "Champagne Charlie" because he often showed up to Parliament
drunk. This is just after the Boston Tea Party, and Townshend says
England needs to keep troops in America because of the bad behavior of
the colonists. He proposes the Townshend Acts—taxes on many goods—
so that the colonists have to fund the army to patrol their own "bad"
behavior.*

*I had a girl who was having a hard time navigating this concept, so
we went the route of what could happen in a school. I told her that this*

was as if all the students were protesting against rules they didn't like enacted by the principal, so a teacher proposed that we have police on campus to keep the students in order, then started charging students for paper, pencils, and other supplies in order to pay the police. She clicked on that quickly, and it became a way for the rest of us in the class to relate to that issue.

—Ellen Berg

Math

Two-step operations. I have an easel with a hand-drawn picture of a hairy leg (just for attention) with a sock and shoe on. One leg is sufficient. I liken solving a two-step operation with variables to putting on and taking off shoes and socks. In the morning you get up and you put on your sock first, then your shoe and you're good for the day. At night when you are getting ready for bed, you don't do the same. You don't take your sock off first. No! You have to undo first what you did last.

When solving a two-step equation, the order of operations (PEMDAS) explains how to do a problem. But when solving for a variable such as $3m + 12 = 27$, then you have to "undo" the addition or subtraction first, before you can undo the multiplication or division, because it was the last thing you did to solve the problem.

—Mary Beth Runyon

Research Papers

I had students explain to me in detail what they had to do: write a research paper on any topic of their choosing, but they had to have a thesis statement to prove. It took a while because it was their first time doing this.

Then I asked them if that assignment reminded them or made them think of anything else they knew of or had done outside of school. It took some questioning by me and prodding, but the first of two classes caught on rather quickly. We had, "It was like cooking a meal—planning it out—lots of parts, you want it all to come out at the same time." Also, " [It was] like life's journey—learning new things, moving for-

*ward, number of stages in life like the stages in a research paper."
Someone compared it to doing a puzzle where all the pieces have to
come together: "I do the outside first, like an outline, and then the inside
fits together, and if one piece is off, then it doesn't fit together right,"
and, "It's like a building that needs structure and needs a strong foundation"—with prompting, we decided that the foundation would be the
thesis statement.*

*This was fascinating for me, and energizing. I asked this class if
this was helpful to them, and they responded positively. This class is
outspoken and honest. They would have told me if they felt it was a
waste. They said it helped them in breaking down the parts of the
research project by relating it to something they already understood and
knew about.*

*Here's another application of metaphors to research papers: Below-
grade-level readers in my urban middle school have a great deal of difficulty doing research. Their answer when assigned to do "a report," is to
come to the media center and copy verbatim everything in the encyclopedia article or whatever source they have located, be it Internet, print,
or whatever. . . . To try to get the students to understand why it isn't necessary to copy everything in the articles, I use a comparison to a supermarket. I ask them if everything in the supermarket is useful, and we
discuss this, with the usual conclusion being that it is, but we don't buy
everything all the time. Then I ask them why they don't buy everything
each time they go and how they determine what to buy when they go
with their parents. Someone usually mentions that they have a list.
From that point on, I lead a discussion about how whatever their teachers have asked for is their "shopping list" for their research, and they
should just read for that information and write it down in note format.
It sometimes helps them to understand that copying everything is a
wasteful endeavor.*

—Cathy Kinzler

Science

*I recently asked a second-grade class to explain their thoughts on the rela-
tionship between science and math . . . are the subjects like brothers, or
brothers and sisters, or cousins? I was most impressed by the conversation.*

—Jon Hanbury

My kids struggle with thinking that chemical and physical properties are things that should interest them. So I talk for quite a while about how they organize their closet. Some of them use types of clothing; others use color of clothing. We don't count throwing everything on the floor as a system! Once we've talked about this, I transition into categorizing elements with their physical/chemical properties. When they've used the closet example, it makes more sense to them that with 100+ elements, scientists and other people needed a system for grouping them. Otherwise everything would just be one heap of dirty clothes in the middle of the room.

—Marsha Ratzel

A car analogy works well for me when teaching about the importance of good nutrition. For example, carbohydrates are like fuel. Sugars burn fast and give the body quick bursts of speed such as fuel injectors and gasoline do for cars when drag-racing. If we want sustained life, i.e., longer drives, however, we'll need to consume slow-to-digest complex carbohydrates to maintain our endurance, and we'll have to match their amount with our needs. Proteins, vitamins, and minerals are necessary for maintaining and repairing body parts, just as a car's transmission, brakes, and window-washing fluids keep the car running—though just like with proteins, vitamins, and minerals, you can have too much of a good thing and need to monitor your levels of each.

Fat is one source of the body's stored fuel tanks, just as we have gas in tanks in cars. We can have too much here as well: In an emergency it's nice to have the fuel, but do we really want to haul all that around just in case? Additionally, as our bodies need exercise to keep things working well, our cars need to be driven, rarely letting their engines sit idle. We "warm up" by stretching before exercising, and we take the time to "warm up" car engines, especially before racing them. Of course, in both human bodies and in cars, extreme exercising or driving can cause major damage.

—Susan Graham

In life science when teaching about DNA, I have asked students to visualize a zipper opening. As the two halves of the zipper separate, they are like the two halves of the DNA double helix, which also opens. Floating around the zipper there are loose zipper teeth, which line up along the now empty zipper halves, and form two complete zippers. The DNA strands are similar, in that they collect loose adenine, thymine, cytosine or guanine molecules, and align them opposite their partners to make pairs—kind of like the opposite teeth in the zipper. It is not a perfect analogy, but it seems to help a bit.

—Anthony Cody

When teaching grade 8 science I get my students to remember the four points to the particle model of matter by comparing it to a middle school dance.

1. Point one states that all matter is made of tiny particles just like a middle school dance is made up of many students.

2. At the dance, the music starts playing and the students start moving and vibrating just like point two in the particle model of matter that states the tiny particles of matter are always moving and vibrating.

3. Then in the dance (the part that I dread and the reason most grade 8 boys even bother attending), a slow song comes on and, well, you know what happens . . . point three states that the particles in matter may be attracted to each other or bonded together.

4. This is the part of the dance where the teachers get involved with their rulers in hand to make sure that point four is occurring. Point four states that the particles have spaces between them. The students get a kick out of it and every dance for the rest of the year they ask me if I am going to have my ruler with me.

—Riley Ellis-Toddington

The way DNA helps to pass along genetic information is often very abstract for students. Often, DNA is referred to as the recipe for proteins. I think that comparison is far too basic. I describe DNA to my students as the "genetic cookbook." First, this idea lends itself well to explaining how genetic information is combined. A cookbook contains recipes from many different places. In the "genetic cookbook" you get half your recipes from your mother's side of the family, and half from your father's. That also allows me to explain that as long as there is a recipe for meat loaf in the cookbook, it doesn't matter if it's your mom's meat loaf or your dad's meat loaf. Similarly, as long as you have a functional version of each gene, it doesn't matter if it came from your mother or your father.

Next, I explain how someone other than you might be interested in making something from the cookbook. If your friend Harold wants to make your mom's meat loaf, you don't have to copy the entire cookbook, just the meat loaf recipe. In the same way, when a protein is being made, the entire cookbook doesn't have to be copied. The individual recipe is like the section of DNA that codes for a certain protein. Once the recipe is copied, it doesn't matter what Harold does with it, you still have the original and can make as many copies as necessary. The copy of the recipe is similar to RNA, as it may be on different paper from the original, but it still bears many similar characteristics of its DNA counterpart. The RNA (copied recipe) is then sent to the ribosome (Harold) where the code is read, and a protein (meat loaf) is made.

The protein made from a section of DNA has specific instructions that must be followed for it to function correctly. Tiny changes in the steps for making the protein can drastically alter the function of that protein. I compare this to exchanging one white powder for another in the making of dad's pound cake recipe in the cookbook. The particular white powder is very important when making a pound cake, as exchanging a cup of salt for a cup of sugar or flour can have drastic effects on the taste of the resulting cake. A switch that doesn't sound terrible to begin with can make a huge difference in the final result.

—Todd Williamson

When the butterflies my students were raising emerged from their chrysalides . . . we would have a butterfly birthday party, complete with party foofers, which unroll when you blow into them in much the same way the butterfly unrolls its proboscis.

—Gail V. Ritchie

When I'm teaching the parts of a plant and their functions in first and second grade, I describe the stem as a straw that sucks the water from the roots to bring it up to the leaves.

—Annette Romano

Standards

When a cabinet maker is faced with a new project, he or she knows that cabinets must:

1. Hang on the wall
2. Open and close

3. *Be situated on a level line*
4. *Hold stuff*

Fortunately, cabinet makers make use of these standards as the minimal parameters for their work. From a variety of raw materials, they craft different and unique products. They add detail. They complicate, amplify, and beautify.

A cabinet maker who didn't go beyond the standard, however, would produce unnoticed, unwanted, and unpurchased work. We teachers must decide to go beyond the standards, even if they're used by the public and the government to assess our progress. The metaphor helps me think through grading situations.

—Wade Whitehead

Students' Perceptions of Self

In 1990 a former elementary school student of mine ended up at my daughters' high school. Within weeks he killed himself with a gun. School officials responded by calling in an outside expert to speak to students and parents. I wish I still knew his name. Anyway, my daughters encouraged me to hear him speak, and he used a metaphor that I have used every year since with my own students.

In effect, each of us is a bubble. On the outside we have many pressures that threaten to burst our bubble. (Kids will brainstorm parents, school, teachers, friends, etc.) We also have on the inside many resources to help our bubbles stay strong. (Again, kids will brainstorm parents, school, teachers, friends, etc.) It always generates a thoughtful discussion that helps students to understand they are not alone and do have others they can turn to in times of crisis.

One year I used this metaphor with a class I had to cover for another teacher. I then asked them to write a reaction to our discussion. One boy told me about his sixth-grade brother who, he felt, was close to committing suicide, as he himself had been the year before. I was able to get counseling resources to both boys because of this metaphor, so I value it.

—Kathie Marshall

Teaching

Here's something I've stolen from somebody: When talking (or maybe ranting a little bit) to school people about the need for interdisciplinary/interconnected learning from a kid's perspective, I talk about if American high schools taught people how to fish we'd have a class about line, a class about reels, a class about rods, and a class about bait, the gifted kids would learn about artificial lures, we'd spend a lot of time learning about boats and water clarity, you get the idea. Anyhow, we'd do this to the kids for four years, make them write term papers on how to fish, and at the end pronounce them fishermen without them ever having been to the lake or putting a hook in the water. Then we talk about how you really teach someone to fish.

—Sid Tanner

I am sure you all have heard of the tale called "Stone Soup." That is what we make here every day. Each of us can come to this network and drop our magic stone into a simmering pot of water. We may muse how good our "idea broth" would be if only we had a bit of this or bit of that. Soon enough our soup is thick and rich with meat, spices, and life-sustaining veggies. Like the ancient tale, every time I throw my stone in I come away well fed and ready to face the world.

—Ellen Holmes

After raising butterflies, my students loved the metaphor of butterfly soup, which represents the stage in metamorphosis when the caterpillar dissolves but the butterfly has not yet formed. We (kids and adults) started noticing that stage in our learning process—the time in between what you knew and what you are coming to know or before you understand a new idea or skill. Or in the writing process, the time when you're finding what you want to say and how to say it; you have to, as the kids said, "just sit in the soup."

—Marjorie Larner

Years ago, a teaching colleague described her most challenging high school English class—filled with moody students who could carry on delightful conversations or be mulishly silent depending on the day or topic. She told me, "On the good days, it's wonderful. On bad days, it's like dragging an elephant through tar." What a perfect metaphor for teaching or collaboration that is going oh-so-slowly, when we feel like we are pulling others along against their will . . . When we struggle to explain what something is, we often are moved to explain what it is like. And in making the connection between disparate items or experiences, we gain new understanding.

—Brenda Power, 2008

Teaching New Teachers

This morning I met my new class of university students in my microteaching class, where we'll work on designing and teaching specific lessons this semester before they go out to student teach in the fall. I wore my life vest and talked about how I'm like the guide in the raft on the whitewater trip. They're going to need to do the paddling and the steering (it wouldn't be much of an experience if they didn't get to do that), and I'll be here to facilitate the trip, share my knowledge of the river 'cause I've been down it a few times before (although I don't know exactly what it'll be like this time), and try to help them avoid any fatal mistakes. We're all in the boat together, we'll probably have to correct some mistakes, and we'll know more at the end of the trip than we do now. Some students liked the analogy and refer to it later in their lesson reflections.

—Laurie Stenehjem

Additional Resources

⚡ Choice Literacy. 2008. "What It's Like."
http://www.choiceliteracy.com/public/541.cfm.
Great for looking at varied approaches to using metaphors for teaching.

⚡ Exploratree. 2007. "Ready-Made Guides."
http://exploratree.org.uk/explore/templates.php.
Great for graphic organizers and other ways to organize thinking.

⚡ Grothe, Dr. Mardy. 2008. *I Never Metaphor I Didn't Like: A Comprehensive Compilation of History's Greatest Analogies, Metaphors, and Similes.* New York: HarperCollins.
This is page after page of great metaphors and analogies from different moments in history and society. It's a wonderful source for discussion starters or looking at multiple perspectives.

⚡ Lakoff, George. 1994. "Conceptual Metaphor Home Page."
http://cogsci.berkeley.edu/lakoff.
The go-to source for conceptual metaphors and metaphor research.

⚡ Provenzo, Eugene F. Jr. et al. 1989. "Metaphor and Meaning in the Language of Teachers." *Teachers College Record* 90(4): 551. *Excellent article on how teachers use metaphors to describe who they are and what they do.*

⚡ Sheehan, Rachel T. 2005. *Negation of Metaphor: A Psycholinguistic Study.* https://www.cs.tcd.ie/courses/csll/sheehart0405.pdf. *This is an interesting research study that cautions teachers against using negated metaphors, such as the examples provided at the end of Chapter 1, because students may have a difficult time understanding the meaning. This is worth consideration, but there are limitations to the study. My experience has shown that, given the right preparation, students respond to negated metaphors quite well.*

⚡ Wallace, Robert M. 2005. "Making Mistakes, Creating Metaphors." *English Leadership Quarterly* 27(3): 10–11. *This is a short article describing a teacher's behind-the-scenes thinking about metaphors in a lesson.*

References

Allen, Linda, and LeAnn Nickelsen. 2008. *Making Words Their Own: Building Foundations for Powerful Vocabularies*. Peterborough, NH: Crystal Springs Books.

Benjamin, Amy. 2005. *Writing in the Content Areas*. 2nd ed. Larchmont, NY: Eye on Education.

Bullock, James. 1994. "Literacy in the Language of Mathematics." *American Mathematical Monthly* 101 (8): 735–743.

Campbell, Duncan. 2009. "Stumped by Curveballs." *The Guardian*, January 19. Available online at www.guardian.co.uk/commentisfree/2009/jan/19/baseball-metaphor-media.

Chandler, Raymond. 1992. *Farewell, My Lovely*. New York: Random House.

Covey, Stephen R. 1990. *The 7 Habits of Highly Effective People*. New York: Simon and Schuster.

Crawford, James, and Stephen Krashen. 2007. *English Learners in American Classrooms: 101 Questions, 101 Answers*. New York: Scholastic.

Danesi, Marcel. 2004. *Poetic Logic: The Role of Language in Thought, Language, and Culture*. Madison, WI: Atwood.

Dictionary.com Unabridged (v 1.1). 2009. S.v., "epiphany." http://dictionary.reference.com/browse/epiphany.

Feldman, Jerome. 2008. *From Molecule to Metaphor: A Neural Theory of Language*. Cambridge, MA: MIT Press.

Fussell, Paul. 2000. *The Great War and Modern Memory*. New York: Oxford University Press.

Gallagher, Kelly. 2004. *Deeper Reading: Comprehending Challenging Texts, 4–12*. Portland, ME: Stenhouse.

Glucksberg, Sam. 2001. *Understanding Figurative Language, From Metaphors to Idioms*. New York: Oxford University Press.

Gordon, William J. 1971. *Synectics: The Development of Creative Capacity*. New York: Collier Books.

Hancewicz, Euthecia, Loretta Heuer, Diana Metsisto, and Cynthia L. Tuttle. 2005. *Literacy Strategies for Improving Mathematics Instruction*. Alexandria, VA: Association for Supervision and Curriculum Development.

Harrison, Allan, and Richard Coll, eds. 2008. *Using Analogies in Middle and Secondary Science*. Thousand Oaks, CA: Corwin.

Hill, Jane D., and Kathleen M. Flynn. 2006. *Classroom Instruction That Works for English Language Learners*. Alexandria, VA: Association for Supervision and Curriculum Development.

Huxley, Thomas H. 1854. "On the Educational Value of the Natural History Sciences." In *Science and Education: Essays*. New York: D. Appleton.

Information Aesthetics. "Paper-Based Visualization Competition: The Winner and More." http://infosthetics.com/archives/2009/02/paperbased_visualization_competition_the_winner_and_more.html.

Koch, Kenneth. 2000. *Wishes, Lies, and Dreams: Teaching Children to Write Poetry*. New York: Harper.

Kovecses, Zoltan. 2002. *Metaphor: A Practical Introduction*. New York: Oxford University Press.

Krashen, Stephen D., and Tracy D. Terrell. 1983. *The Natural Approach: Language Acquisition in the Classroom*. Hayward, CA: Alemany Press.

Lakoff, George. 1994. "Conceptual Metaphor Home Page." http://cogsci.berkeley.edu/lakoff.

Lakoff, George, and Mark Johnson. 1980. *Metaphors We Live By*. Chicago: University of Chicago Press.

Linder, Douglas O. 2008. "State v. John Scopes (The 'Monkey Trial')." http://www.law.umkc.edu/faculty/projects/ftrials/scopes/evolut.htm.

Marzano, Robert. 2001. *Classroom Instruction That Works: Research-Based Strategies for Increasing Student Achievement*. Alexandria, VA: Association for Supervision and Curriculum Development.

Merriam-Webster. 2004. *Merriam-Webster's Collegiate Dictionary*. 11th ed. Springfield, MA: Merriam Webster.

Orwell, George. 1946. "Politics and the English Language." Available online at http://orwell.ru/library/essays/politics/English/e_polit.

Pinar, William et al. 1995. *Understanding Curriculum: An Introduction to the Study of Historical and Contemporary Critical Discourses* (Counterpoints, Vol. 17). New York: Peter Lang.

Pink, Daniel H. 2005. *A Whole New Mind: Moving from the Information Age to the Conceptual Age*. New York: Riverhead Books.

Pinker, Steven. 2007. *The Stuff of Thought: Language as a Window Into Human Nature*. New York: Viking.

Power, Brenda. 2008. "The Big Fresh: What It's Like." *Choice Literacy*. http://www.choiceliteracy.com/public/541.cfm.

Provenzo, Eugene F., Jr. 1989. "Metaphor and Meaning in the Language of Teachers." *Teachers College Record* 90 (4): 551.

Safire, William. 2008. "Metaphor Mix." *New York Times Sunday Magazine*, Oct. 26.

ScienceDaily. 2009. "Visual Learners Convert Words to Pictures in the Brain and Vice Versa, Says Psychology Study." *ScienceDaily*, March 28. Available online at http://www.sciencedaily.com/releases/2009/03/090325091834.htm, University of Pennsylvania.

Sontag, Susan. 1978. *Illness as a Metaphor*. New York: Farrar, Straus, and Giroux.

Sousa, David. 2005. *How the Brain Learns*. 3rd ed. Thousand Oaks, CA: Corwin.

Stanish, Bob. 1990. *Mindanderings*. Carthage, IL: Good Apple.

Starko, Alane. 2000. *Creativity in the Classroom: Schools of Curious Delight*. 2nd ed. Mahwah, NJ: Lawrence Erlbaum.

Strauss, Stephen. 2009. "We Need a Satisfactory Metaphor for DNA." *New Scientist*, February 23. Available online at http://www.newscientist.com/article/mg20126965.800-seeking-a-satisfactory-metaphor-for-dna.html.

Talk of the Nation: Science Friday, with Ira Flatow, April 3, 2009.

Thompson, Terry. 2008. *Adventures in Graphica: Using Comics and Graphic Novels to Teach Comprehension, 2–6*. Portland, ME: Stenhouse.

Thoreau, Henry David. 1995. *Walden* (annotated ed.). Boston: Houghton Mifflin.

Tomlinson, Carol Ann. 2008. *Connecting Differentiated Instruction, Understanding by Design, and What Works in Schools: An Exploration of Research-Based Strategies*. DVD. Alexandria, VA: Association for Supervision and Curriculum Development.

Twain, Mark. 1903. "Was the World Made for Man?" Quoted at http://www.twainquotes.com/Evolution.html.

Van Dyke, Frances. 1998. *A Visual Approach to Algebra*. Palo Alto, CA: Dale Seymour.

Wallace, Robert. 2005. "Making Mistakes, Creating Metaphors." *English Leadership Quarterly* 27 (3): 10–11.

Wheatley, Margaret. 2006. *Leadership and the New Science: Discovering Order in a Chaotic World*. 3rd ed. San Francisco: Berrett-Koehler.

Williams, Frank. 1983. *Creativity Assessment Packet*. Austin, TX: PRO-ED.

Wormeli, Rick. 2001. *Meet Me in the Middle: Becoming an Accomplished Middle-Level Teacher*. Portland, ME: Stenhouse.

———. 2005. *Summarization in Any Subject*. Alexandria, VA: Association for Supervision and Curriculum Development.

———. 2009. "Emancipating the English Language Learner." *Middle Ground* 12 (4): 41–42.

Index